WOODEN BOAT DESIGNS

WOODEN BOAT DESIGNS

Classic Danish Boats
measured and described by
CHRISTIAN NIELSEN

Translated from the Danish by Erik J. Friis

Foreword by Jonathan Wilson, Editor of *WoodenBoat* Magazine

CHARLES SCRIBNER'S SONS ◆ NEW YORK

The original Danish edition of *Wooden Boat Designs* was published by Høst & Søns Forlag, Copenhagen, in cooperation with Handels og Søfartsmuseet (Museum of Commerce and Maritime History) at Kronborg Castle, in whose series "Publications on Maritime History" this volume appeared as No. VII. The many drawings are the work of Christian Nielsen. Mr. Palle Christiansen conceived the idea of the book and wrote the text on the basis of Christian Nielsen's descriptive material and his own studies. We acknowledge with thanks the contribution of Erik J. Friis, who translated the book from the Danish.

Front of jacket: A decked Sound boat pulled up on shore. This vessel was probably used as a pilot boat or a large bumboat.

Frontispiece: A Kattegat boat on shore; pencil drawing from one of Chr. Blache's sketchbooks. The artist has left out the bulwarks on both sides but has included a pencil sketch of a ketch, whose rigging partly juts out over the Kattegat boat.

Translated from the original Danish by Erik J. Friis
English translation copyright © Stanford Maritime 1980

Originally published as DANSKE BÅDTYPER: OPMÅLT OG BESKREVET AF CHRISTIAN NIELSEN
Copyright © Høst & Søns Forlag, Copenhagen 1977

First U.S. edition published 1980

Library of Congress Cataloging in Publication Data

Nielsen, Christian, 1914–
    Wooden boat designs.

    1. Boat-building.   2. Boats and boating.
3. Ships, Wooden.   4. Naval architecture.   I. Title.
VM321.N55   623.8′207   80-13917
ISBN 0-684-16432-9

1 3 5 7 9 11 13 15 17 19   V/C   20 18 16 14 12 10 8 6 4 2

Printed in the United States of America

CONTENTS

FOREWORD vii

INTRODUCTION ix

MAP xiii

"BUILD ME A BOAT" 1

I.
HERRING BOATS 13
    The Nordenhuse Boat *Hejmdal* 15
    The Kerteminde Boat *Ruth* 19

THE SOUND BOATS 21
    The Sound Boat *Thora* 23
    The Isefjord Boat *Maries Minde* 27

THE BORNHOLM BOATS 29
    The Bornholm Boat *Haabet* 31

THE ACCEPTANCE OF THE MOTOR 34
    The Lohals Boat *Victoria* 37
    The Nyborg Boat *Helga* 39

THE FORMATION OF FISHERMEN'S ORGANIZATIONS 41
    The Spritsail Boat from Snekkersten 43
    The Stern Boat *Odin* 47
    The Double-ended Boat *Jens* 49

II.
SPRITSAIL CRAFT 51
    Three-masted Spritsail Craft from Aarø 55
    Two-masted Spritsail Craft from Eckernförde 57
    Two-masted Spritsail Craft from Halmø 59

III.
SAILING DRIFTERS 61
    The German Drifter *Minna* 65
    The Fejø Sailing Drifter *De 13 Søskende* 69

IV.

FJORD BOATS 70
   Flatner from the Limfjord 73
   Flatner from Løgstør 77
   The Skiff *Lilly* 79
   The Glyngøre Boat *Støren* 81
   Flatner from Slien 83
   Flatner from Orø 85
   Dinghy from Lynæs 87

V.

NORTH SEA BOATS 90
   Pram from Hjerting 99
   Pram from Vorupør 101
   Skiff from Klitmøller 105
   Oceangoing Boat from Hvide Sande 107
   Spritsail Boat from Løkken 109
   The Beach Pram *Marie* 111

THE EXPANSION OF THE FISHERIES 113
   The Cutter *Gorm* 115
   A Danish Seine Boat 119

IMPROVED COASTAL VESSELS 120
   The Coastal Boat *Viking* 123
   The Coastal Boat *Bent* 125

VI.

SAILING COASTERS 127
   The Sailing Barge *Metta Catharina* 135
   The Sloop *De Fire Brødre* 137
   Flatboat from Løkken 141
   Flatner from Randers 143
   The Sloop *Castor* 145

VII.

SERVICE BOATS 147
   Customs Sloop *XXVII* 153
   Pilot Boat *Helsingør* 155
   Spritsail Bumboat from Dragør 159
   Iceboat from the Great Belt 161

FOREWORD

THE TRADITIONAL WORKING CRAFT OF THE INTRICATE coasts on the globe have long held most of us in utter fascination. Designed from experience and built with good sense, they are beautiful examples of the blending of form and function, and their history and evolution have influenced much of the thinking in work- and pleasure-boat design today.

Yet, even that influence has become distilled, as new generations of builders and designers take their places in history, influenced in part by a generation that itself followed after the age of working sail. In our own clumsy ways, we struggle to discover the links that will span those generations, to reconnect with the roots and the branches of thought and experience.

Our museums do much to inspire those links, with their models, their boats, their plans and drawings, and musty record books. For many, these things are the doorways to the past, and for all it would be a duller world without them. But even the best run among them have a difficult time communicating the meaning of their collections: the interrelationship of diverse boat types, the specific needs that inspired their creation, and the powerful genius that was expressed through their design and construction.

There was a time when all boats were conceived in experience, and built by hand and eye alone—without models or drawings, but from the knowledge and good sense that had passed through generations of hardworking and resourceful people. They understood the demands of the sea and the potential of the wood that they shaped and fitted with such reverence and precision. There are still artisans to be found who practice that ancient art, and most of them are found in the distant fjords and quiet coves of Scandinavia's coasts, where the roots of contemporary practice evolved. The legends of the Vikings and their ships are filled with wonder for sailors, adventurers, and boatbuilders. Yet, too often we think only of Norway and Sweden when we listen to the legends and conjure great dreams. Too often we forget about Denmark, a country whose craft are unique and whose heritage continues to influence design in our own country.

It is no small miracle that the precise and tireless work of Christian Nielsen has been preserved and collected, and that the publishers should see fit to share that work in this country, for there is much to be learned from it. In the following pages will be found a wealth of experience and information. The unique and distinctive wooden boats of the coasts of Denmark, their history, purpose, and evolution are explored and discussed in a way that lets them speak for themselves. In the process, another link is forged and our world becomes larger, our understanding greater.

It is an invitation to pay attention to the works of others, who paid attention themselves, and who, in turn, gave us beautiful, functional craft with which to wrest a living and a future from the sea.

—Jonathan Wilson
Editor, *WoodenBoat* Magazine

INTRODUCTION

DURING WORLD WAR I, THE DANISH FISHERIES EXPERI-
enced a great economic boom as a result of the increasing demand for
food. For the fishermen it was a long-awaited opportunity to improve
not only the gear and equipment but the vessels themselves. Thus, as
the war years passed, the traditional boats of the Danish coasts were replaced. In some places the fishermen would retain the simple, local,
and—most important—inexpensive designs, and were, in the main, sat-
isfied with the necessary changes in the layout and motor size required
by the new technology. Others dared to make the leap represented by
the acquisition of the new and powerful cutters, built according to entirely different principles from those upon which the older vessels had
been constructed. But the old boats were not abandoned in the process.
The smaller craft might end up in fjords and bays, but very often would
remain where they had always been—used now by older fishermen going
out on an occasional fishing trip. The decked boats were often sold to
fishermen who frequented more sheltered waters, where a need had developed for bigger boats, but not necessarily cutters.

Curiously enough, even as these dramatic changes were taking place,
the living standard of the fishing population remained very modest; economic security did not become a reality until the next generation.

At that time (the late 1930s), the Danish Maritime Museum at Kronborg Castle, near Helsingør, began to register all these older types of
boats, since it was thought that they were about to disappear. The ini-
tiative was taken by the then Director of the Museum, Knud Klem, and
by Knud E. Hansen, the museum's consultant on maritime technology.
The acquisition and transportation of the boats were both beyond the fi-
nancial and spatial means of the museum, but with support forthcoming
from the Tuborg Fund, it became possible to effect the next-best solu-
tion: to measure and describe characteristic boat types, in the field. The
task was entrusted to a young boatbuilder named Christian Nielsen.

Nielsen, whose ancestors lived on the island of Fejø, comes from a
long line of boatbuilders and, prior to the project, had taken several
courses in naval architecture given by Knud E. Hansen. He established,
by means of preliminary measurements, a very accurate and time-saving

method of recording, which he carried out during his vacations until 1953, when he was employed as builder of ship models and curator at the Maritime Museum, where he was then able to complete his working drawings.

Each summer his recording work would concentrate on a certain sector of the coastline, and he slowly worked his way along the map of Denmark. The work would proceed, for instance, along the west coast of Jutland (lasting two summers) with Nielsen, his gear, his baggage, and his bicycle, first traveling by train to one of the most distant places on his itinerary (Frederikshavn at the northern tip of Jutland), and from there by bicycle south along the coast, stopping in each little hamlet. The local boats were described and measured, and their owners were interviewed, before he would continue his journey.

The recording, which took between 10 and 15 years, went on according to plan. In all, about 80 vessels were measured. Later on, a number of additional vessels were measured, so that the grand total is now about 100. By going through the finished drawings, we have found that there are certain gaps in the geographical coverage of the Danish coastline. However, the museum is aware of the types that are still missing and need to be measured; it is hoped that the work will be completed before long.

A number of communications from both Denmark and abroad have confirmed the staff of the Maritime Museum in their belief that this work of measuring and recording is very valuable. Being an active documentation center, the museum has for a long time been desirous of making this material available to a larger readership.

It would have been preferable to present a carefully prepared collection of drawings, all of them placed in a social, geographic, and contemporary context, but that has not been possible because of a lack of money, time, and expertise. Instead, the museum has decided to publish a representative selection of the drawings, to which has been added a brief but factual text, in addition to brief essays about the spread and distribution of different types of boats and their uses.

The preparation of this material for publication was begun in 1968 and has been the work of Christian Nielsen and Palle Christiansen, a boatbuilder, under the supervision of Knud Klem and Dr. Henning Henningsen. Museum inspector Ole Crumlin-Pedersen, who is also the Maritime Museum's technical consultant, has participated in the preparatory work prior to the publication of this book.

The purpose of the book is to offer the public the lines and construction drawings of a selection of smaller and characteristically Danish boats of the period 1870 to 1930. The selection is meant to be a reflection of the diversity in form and type among vessels that, as far as the museum is aware, has been in use in Danish waters during that period. The growing interest on the part of the public in regard to the investigation and restoration of old boats has also confirmed the practical utility of our work.

The arrangement of the boats selected for publication has been revised to try to distribute the forty-one measurement projects, each of which consists of two or three drawings, into different sections in such a way that each section appears as a harmonious unit.

At first we attempted a regional grouping, with the boats being classified according to the area in which they had been used or for which they had been built. However, this grouping didn't provide any natural divisions as far as the construction and use of the vessels were concerned. Since this method also mingled large and small boats having no close relationship with each other, we felt that the regional division of this material was not very useful.

An attempt was then made to classify the vessels according to type on a historical-geographical basis. We selected six different structural types as indicators, then distributed all the special characteristics of the boats onto six different distribution cards, according to where each vessel had been used and/or built. This method provided us with a very diffuse picture of the spread and distribution of the different types, and with few exceptions there were no clear trends indicating any larger and well-defined groups.

There were many reasons for this poor result. First, there was not enough material and it was collected haphazardly, and, second, it was too concerned with the earliest time periods. In addition, boats, in contrast to buildings, are ever on the move, and the question arises whether they are to be classified according to the locality of their construction or of their use. In sum, it was found that there were ample reasons for not proceeding with a classification based on historical-geographical factors.

We then tried to arrive at a sensible grouping based on use. Slowly, we attempted to sort out the principles underlying the multiplicity of methods utilized by fishermen during the sixty years in question. Subsequently, the main fisheries were divided according to technology and the waters in which the fishing took place, and the vessels were grouped according to the kind of fishery in which they had been used. When the measurements had been adjusted in the light of this system, it was interesting to find that there were great similarities and quite a few paradoxes. In spite of the paradoxes, however, there was no doubt as to the correctness of this method of classification. Differences in type and size within each individual fishery were of especial interest.

The classification of the vessels according to their everyday use thus became the basis for the presentation of this material. With certain exceptions, the pieces in this otherwise very difficult material fell into place and made up fairly uniform units. The text on the following pages has become somewhat longer than planned because of this method of arranging the material. In each section, the various types of fisheries and the kinds of boats used will be dealt with. We have found that the type of fishery, whether deep-sea or coastwise, has had a direct influence on the design of the boats involved, and this again has served to divide the activities of the fishermen. These factors, together with geographical, social, and developmental circumstances, have contributed to the fashioning of the most important industry of the coastal population of Denmark—the fisheries.

The text presents the various boat types in a context of production and development, but it is the many drawings that are the actual core of the book. As the years go on, we will gain more knowledge about these boats, and our accompanying text will no doubt have to be revised in the future.

In order to provide a clear picture of these wooden boats, we have tried to obtain a suitable photograph of each boat measured. In some cases, these photos are actual pictures of the boats concerned, but in other cases they are pictures of similar vessels. In certain cases we have been able to provide artistic renditions of typical boats through contemporary sketches, pictures, or woodcuts, which depict the boats in use, and most of this material has been obtained from the large collections of the Maritime Museum.

Palle Christiansen

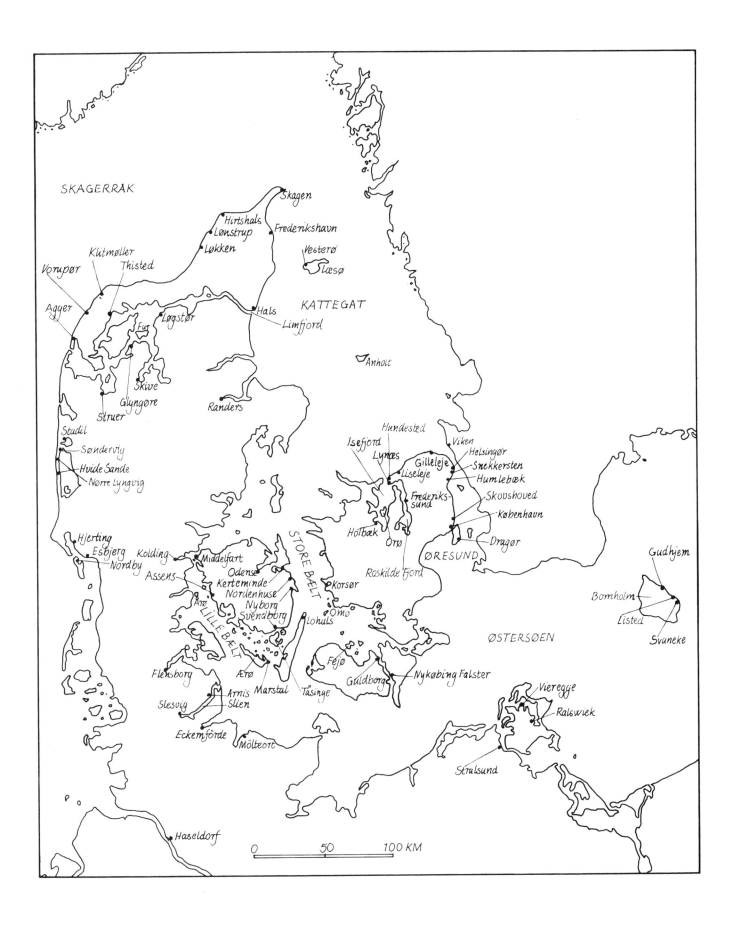

SKAGERRAK

Skagen

Hirtshals
Lønstrup
Løkken
Frederikshavn

Vesterø
Læsø

KATTEGAT

Klitmøller
Thisted
Vorupør
Agger
Løgstør
Hals
Limfjord

Fur

Studil
Skive
Glyngøre
Struer
Randers

Anholt

Søndervig
Hvide Sande
Nørre Lyngvig

Hundested
Isefjord
Lynæs
Viken
Helsingør
Gilleleje
Snekkersten
Liseleje
Humlebæk
Frederikssund
Skovshoved
København
Holbæk
Orø
Dragør
Raskilde Fjord
ØRESUND

Hjerting
Esbjerg
Nordby
Kolding
Middelfart
STORE BÆLT
Odense
Kerteminde
Assens
Nordenhuse
Korsør
Atø
Nyborg
Svendborg
Omø
LILLEBÆLT
Lohals

Gudhjem
Bomholm
Listed
Svaneke

ØSTERSØEN

Flensborg
Ærø
Marstal
Tåsinge
Fejø
Guldborg
Nykøbing Falster

Arnis
Slesvig
Slien
Viereggie
Ralswiek

Eckemförde
Mölteort

Haseldorf

Stralsund

0   50   100 KM

"BUILD ME A BOAT"

"HOW MUCH WILL YOU CHARGE TO BUILD ME A BOAT THAT will tack quickly and carry our fish?''

Such questions have long been asked of boatbuilders by fishermen all along the Danish coast. Actually, the fisherman is asking only about the cost, for the question as formed involves a tacit understanding between the two men. The fisherman doesn't specify the boat's length, beam, or shape. He understands that the boatbuilder knows well the type of vessel used for fishing in his part of the country, and only indicates the special attributes he wants his boat to have. He relies on the boatbuilder to apply his needs to the material itself, and in most cases receives just the boat that he had in mind.

Boatbuilders, through generations of experience, have developed methods and materials to suit craft whose uses might vary considerably. Yet, each boatbuilder has, on account of his restricted regional market, limited himself to a small number of boat types, none of which needed any precise explanation.

Boats are generally classified according to whether they have been constructed on a keel, on a plank, or with a flat bottom, and whether they are clinker- or carvel-built. Most smaller boats, at least in Den-

Christian Nielsen's boatbuilding yard on the island of Fejø in 1914. A 41-foot boat intended for the packet service is being planked up. On the left is the boatbuilder's house, with, left to right, the boatbuilder Carl Nielsen, the father of Curator Christian Nielsen; the owner of the new vessel; and Christian Nielsen.

♦ 1

mark, are clinker-built, with the planks overlapping and being riveted together before the ribs or frames are installed. In carvel building, the planks are fitted edge to edge and fastened to the frame timbers, resulting in a vessel with completely smooth sides.

The great majority of boats shown in this book are clinker-built vessels, since in the past only the biggest fishing boats and cargo vessels were carvel-built. How the boatbuilders carried out the actual construction of the boats is not well documented, but it is probable that most of the vessels we have measured were actually built without any construction drawings, for the traditions of the craft and the experience and knowledge of the boatbuilder were the ultimate authority.

Clinker Building by Rule of Thumb

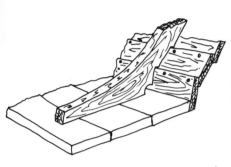

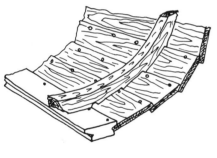

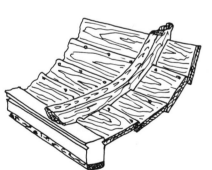

During the years covered in this book, some boatbuilders still applied the ancient method of constructing their vessels without the use of drawings, transferring the intended shape directly to the wood without the intermediate step of patterns or models. The shipbuilder Frode Willumsen tells of how his master, Laurits Svendsen of Snekkersten, built boats at the beginning of the twentieth century:

> As soon as he had fetched the wood from the forest, he split it lengthwise and placed it up against some trees, so that it would dry faster. To shape the stem and sternpost, he found some compass timber that he thought had the right curve, trimmed each to fit, and bolted them to the keel. Then he cut a rabbet along each side of the keel and posts, and set the assembly upright on blocks. By bracing off the posts with laths, he made sure that they were in line. When all was ready, he fitted the garboard [the lowest plank] in place, making sure that it fit well at either end. Then he repeated the process on the other side. For the next plank up, he first selected one that he thought had the right shape, steamed it and clamped it in place over the garboard. When it had taken its shape, he drew a pencil line along its lower edge, cut off the part below that line, shaped the ends, and riveted it in place. Before that he had chiseled a bevel on the upper edge of the plank below to make it fit. He used no molds, but measured the distance from the keel to the upper edge of each plank in order to make the boat symmetrical.
>
> Laurits Svendsen thus built his boats by the rule of thumb only and on the basis of his experience, and his boats were always held in great favor by the fishermen.

Clinker Building with Molds

The method seems simple, but it required a wealth of experience and familiarity with the boats. In order for the reader to better understand the more elaborate drawings in this book, we will briefly describe the building of a decked clinker-built herring boat and a larger carvel-built cutter.

When the fisherman and the boatbuilder have agreed on the price for the vessel, and the length and height of the boat have been decided on, the keel and posts are fashioned and fastened together. The rabbet is cut so that the planks will lie fairly along it, the entire construction set up on a number of blocks, and the stem and sternpost are well braced.

If the boatbuilder is using cross-sectional molds, these are now set up on the keel at the desired spacing. The number of molds may vary—one, three, or five being most usual. When set up, they provide a form over which to bend planks, unlike the more ancient method, where the shape was determined by experienced eye.

The most common procedure in planking the boats is to use a spiling batten, a thin board that roughly follows the shape of the plank. The batten is placed where the new plank is to be attached, and the lower edge is marked off to conform with the top edge of the plank below it. The plank's position on the stem and sternpost and on the molds is noted on the batten. The batten is then taken off and placed on the next plank, where the measurement points are transferred. Lines are then drawn through those points, which are the upper and lower edges of the plank, and it is cut to shape. It is then steamed in a steam box so that it becomes pliable enough to be clamped tightly to the plank already in place, and it is fastened to it with iron or copper rivets. The boatbuilder continues in this manner from the garboard to the sheer strake, the uppermost plank. The way the planks are placed is of great importance to the appearance of the boat, and the boatbuilder will always attempt to obtain a fair or pleasing curve, with planks of uniform width.

When the planking process has been completed, the ribs are set in place. The ribs consist of floor timbers, which are attached to the top of the keel or bottom boards, and the futtocks, which overlap the floor

Lynæs boatbuilder's yard, ca. 1900. Two clinker-built boats for the fisheries in the Kattegat are being planked. In the foreground there are two spruce logs to be used as masts, and in the rear at the right is the house of the boatbuilder.

timbers and to which the planks are fastened. Floor timbers and futtocks may lie side by side or may be spaced out and bolted independently of each other; both methods may even be used by the same boatbuilder. When measuring the ribs, a device is often used which consists of small wooden pieces riveted together to resemble a stiff chain. At the spot where the rib is to be placed, the device is knocked evenly against the side of the vessel, so that it conforms to the shape of the hull. It is then carefully removed, and its shape is transferred by pencil onto the rib stock, which may then be roughly cut into the desired shape. Then, taking it into the boat, the rib is marked exactly to the shape of the inside of the planking and cut accordingly. When that's done, it is ready to be attached to the vessel. In the past, the ribs were fastened to the planking with wooden pins called treenails, but later boatbuilders changed over to iron nails.

When the floor timbers and ribs are in place, the fish well is built. Care is taken when putting floor timbers in place to make two or three of them high enough to provide sufficient space in the well, and strong enough to support the horizontal well deck, which is nailed upon them. A box-shaped hatchway is built above the center of the well deck and made so high that it reaches above the waterline; thus, water cannot splash out of it, even if the boat carries a list when fully loaded. Holes are bored in the planks of the well so that the water will be constantly replenished and provide the fish with oxygen. Trading smacks and boats intended for seine fishing often feature an especially large well, since in their case it is important to keep the fish alive for longer periods.

A gunwale, or sheer clamp, is attached on the inside of the upper edge of the topmost plank; it serves to stiffen the structure and is of the same thickness as the futtocks. It is tied to the ends of the boat by means of breasthooks, which are themselves fastened to the stem and sternpost. The deck beams are joined to the gunwale with nailed straps and placed slightly below it. Gunwales, beams, keel, and posts are as a rule made from oak, while the planking may be of oak, larch, or fir. On the beams are placed deck planks (usually pine), which are fastened to all the whole and half beams with nails.

If the boat is to have a bulwark along its sides, it may be a plank bolted to the gunwale, or several planks set on edge and fastened to the gunwale with iron straps or stanchions. On larger vessels, stanchions are often placed in such a way that they penetrate the gunwale and extend along the inside of the planking. A molding, or cap rail, is often fastened on top of the bulwark.

If the boat is to have a motor, a few strong floor timbers serve as the foundation onto which the motor is fastened. The motor must be in line with the propeller shaft that goes right through the sternpost. Above the motor, a deckhouse is built to contain the various controls. Extending aft from the deckhouse is usually a wheelhouse.

Midship, a low coaming is placed around the cargo hold and the well, both of which are protected by removable hatch covers.

Forward, there is a small deckhouse with a sliding hatch that leads down to a cabin containing two or three bunks in addition to a table and a clothes locker. A small coal-burning stove is also part of the equipment, since the boats are often used for winter fishing out of foreign ports.

The boatbuilder has beforehand purchased long and slender spruce or larch logs to be shaped into a mast, a boom, a gaff, and a jibboom. The rigging is usually done by the boatbuilder himself, but the fittings for the mast, the chain plates for the shrouds, the rudder braces, deck horses (upon which the mainsail boom and jib may move from side to side), and other iron work are forged by the local blacksmith. In addition, there are special fittings, such as lead blocks for lines that may be rigged later, that are not normally included in the delivery price proper.

The painting of the vessel was usually done by the new owner, since he would, as a rule, arrive a few days before the boat was finished. He also assisted in the work of planing smooth the spars, and once in a while he would even cut and sew the sails, since many fishermen had learned this skill while serving on larger sailing vessels.

When the boat was ready for launching, it was pulled down to the beach or the slipway. Men from the town would help with the launching,

A carvel-built fishing cutter being planked. Pen-and-ink drawing from the island of Læsø by Johannes Larsen, 1924.

and the new owner showed his appreciation by throwing a big party. When the vessel had been ballasted, fully rigged, and taken out on its trial run, the owner took over the boat and was given a builder's certificate by the boatbuilder. The builder's certificate, required by the customs administration, contained the boat's name, builder's location, materials used, and the price. When all was in order, the vessel could be registered.

Carvel Building by Rule of Thumb

Smaller boatyards did not possess much in the way of workshop facilities or machinery; indeed, many fishing boats were built on the open beach or in the fisherman's backyard. But in order to build the heavier carvel-planked boats, the larger boatyards required sites that were more developed, with the facilities and equipment to handle the large heavy timbers.

In the very early days, when ship carpenters were not familiar with drawings and plans, many carvel-planked ships were built by rule of thumb, much the same as the clinker-built vessels. It was an arduous method, but the builders managed by adapting many of the techniques they had become accustomed to in constructing clinker boats. When the keel and posts had been put up, they would place three to five pairs of ribs on the keel, spreading them out and fairing them until all lines were smooth and sweet from stem to stern. Even with long experience and a sharp eye, it might still be very difficult to fair everything in, and many builders felt better in putting up a few floor timbers before starting in with the planking.

Since the planks in a carvel-built vessel are not fastened to each other, this technique requires much stouter ribs and a better method of fastening them together than is the case in a clinker-built vessel.

In carvel-built vessels constructed by rule of thumb, most of the ribs have to be fitted and attached after the planks are put in place, making this method of construction too time-consuming and expensive. The method has almost fallen into disuse and is now used only in the building of small dinghies and pleasure craft, which are often planked on forms or molds, after which transverse bent frames are riveted to the planks.

Carvel Building on the Basis of Drawings

Not many boats were built by rule of thumb in the larger yards, for the master boatbuilders there decided on the shape of the vessel on the basis of their practical and theoretical knowledge.

Ship carpenters dubbing (or fairing) the ribs of a carvel-built vessel with adzes. The two uppermost planks and the bulwark are in place. The double ribs, consisting of the floor timber and futtocks, are clearly seen. The space between the futtocks and the spacing between each double rib are also shown.

First, they would make a drawing showing the ship from one side (the sheer plan), another one as seen from above, and two drawings showing the ship from ahead and astern. On the latter, they would draw in the contours of all the ribs, which they had developed generally in the drawing of the sheer plan. To the shipwrights this new drawing, called the body plan, was the most important drawing, since with it and a number of fixed measurements, called offsets, they were able to fill in all the lines in the drawing. The full-sized body plan was lofted onto a large flat wooden platform, or floor, and all the various rib shapes transferred to the timbers from which the ribs were cut.

Patterns are made from the full-sized lines and are used to locate suitable timber. The shape is marked off and the pieces cut and pinned or treenailed together to form a whole rib on the platform. If there are double-sawn ribs, the floor timber and the futtocks are placed on the platform, and on top of these, with a few inches between, is added still another layer of timber, consisting of two futtocks, which are placed across the center of the floor timber. If the shape of the ribs is very curved, another pair of futtocks is attached. The entire construction is then bolted together.

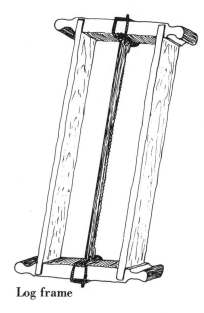

Log frame

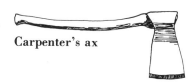

Carpenter's ax

Adze

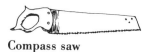

Compass saw

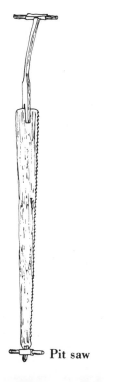

Pit saw

When the first set of ribs is ready, it is hauled from the platform, which is often placed level with the upper edge of the keel, onto the keel, where it is set upright in position and bolted in place. The stem has already been erected, and the work proceeds, as the ribs are constructed, slowly aft, ending at the stern. If the ribs have not already been beveled to conform to the fore-and-aft curve of the ship, the excess wood is dubbed off with an adze.

The vessel now looks like a skeleton of wood with the ribs treenailed or bolted to the keel, reminding the viewer of a human rib cage.

Now the planking can begin. If the vessel is to be completed in a hurry, the two uppermost planks are attached first, so that the other shipwrights may start to put sheer clamps and deck beams in place. Thereupon, the planking team continues the planking process, but they now start from the keel and work upward. Since the planks in carvel-built vessels are always heavier than those in clinker-built boats, it is more difficult to bend them into shape, and it is usually necessary to soften most planks with steam in a steam box, or sweat box, so that they can be twisted into the desired shape. In the distant past, planks used to be scorched over an open fire, while being moistened with water to prevent them from burning. Although this was regarded as a splendid way of making them waterproof, they almost always became a bit charred.

The vessel's keel and the planking below the waterline are often made of beech wood, since this kind of wood is very durable if it is constantly in the water or is kept moist; the planking above the waterline and the stem and sternposts, however, are made from oak, which is less susceptible to rotting and to the spread of fungus.

When the planks are bent and fitted, they are nailed to the ribs, and during the entire planking process, the shipwrights will take care to stagger as much as possible the butts where the plank ends are joined together, so that the planking will be strong and even. When the planking has been completed, the two sides are planed smooth, and the seams are caulked with oakum and later paid with pitch and putty.

If two work gangs have been involved in the construction, sheer clamps have in the meantime been placed at the level of the deck on the inside of the ribs; they run from stem to stern and are one of the most important elements of strength in carvel-built vessels.

Slightly cambered transverse deck beams have been bolted to the uppermost clamp, or shelf, and on top of the beams there is a covering board, or planksheer, along the edge of the deck. On the inside edge of this is a waterway. These heavy members (usually of pine) and the uppermost plank are all bolted together.

Hatches to the cargo hold are mounted, and a forecastle and a hous-

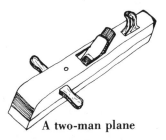

A two-man plane

Smoothing plane

ing for the motor are built. Inner planking, or ceiling, is installed in the cargo hold, and the forecastle will contain accommodations for the crew, with bunks, clothes lockers, and a table. The bed for the motor is placed aft, where it is mounted in the same way as in clinker-built boats.

The wheelhouse is bolted to the motor's deckhouse, and the bulwarks are nailed to the stanchions that rise through the planksheer; the bulwarks are finished with cap rails. When the deck has been caulked and the vessel has been painted and oiled, everything is ready for the launching. It is best to launch the vessel as soon as possible, so that the wood will not dry more than absolutely necessary.

When the ship is in the water, covers and special fittings are made, and the spars are polished and put in place. The rigging of the vessel is completed, and when the steering gear and the capstan are functioning and the navigational instruments have been put in place, the vessel is ready for a trial trip. If the trip is satisfactory in every way, the vessel is delivered with a builder's certificate, which also contains a list of cables, lines, and fishing gear, things that have little to do with the shipyard but which, for the sake of control, are included if the vessel has been built with a government loan.

The Tools

The building of ships and boats has always been a time-consuming craft, and the profit has been small, one of the reasons, perhaps, for the late mechanization of these trades.

Frame saws were not used by the shipyards to cut the big logs that came from the forests until after World War I. Prior to that, the logs were cut into planks with two-man pit saws on large sawhorses, one man on top of the log and another standing below.

Smaller logs were cut with a log frame, which consisted of a big saw blade fastened in the middle of an oblong frame of wood. The stem and the stern were cut with a pit saw, but because of their curved shapes, these parts of the vessel were often placed across a small trench to be sawn, since it would be difficult to balance the piece on two sawhorses. The lower of the two sawyers would then have to stand in the trench to pull the saw.

There was no point in sawing smaller logs, since it was faster to square them with a carpenter's ax. The ribs were cut into shape with a woodsman's ax or a carpenter's ax, and later beveled with an adze.

When the planks had been cut, they were stacked, with small sticks in between, to dry in a place where the wind could get at them. By drying

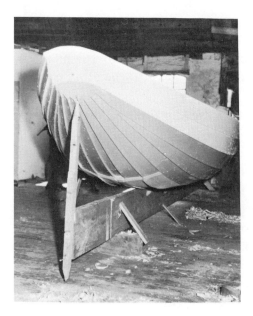

Pram under construction at Eron Andersen's boatyard at North Vorupør. (A pram is a simply built boat. This one could also be called a skiff.) One can clearly see the rounded bottom of the pram and the extra chafing planks on the bottom. Photograph from 1965.

the wood, builders prevented it from shrinking when in place any more than absolutely necessary. When the planks were sufficiently dry and their dimensions indicated, they were squared with a compass saw and planed with a smoothing plane.

When larger pieces were to be planed, shipwrights used a plane operated by two men. Most of the types of work done in the old days with a compass saw were performed after 1910 with a band saw in most places. Such a saw was at first hand operated, but was later driven by a motor. During the first fifty years that the band saw was used in the boatyards, it was often the only mechanical equipment they had. Most of the boatbuilders started out with a used band saw, frequently purchased from a woodworking factory that had obtained more modern equipment; machine tools had been in use in the bigger joiners' workshops since the 1880s, the early years of industrialism in Denmark.

Later the boatbuilders bought planing and joining machines from the joiners' shops. During the interwar period many of the boatbuilders also obtained portable drills, and such tools, together with a band saw and a planer, are often the only machines now seen in a small boatyard. In the larger boatyards and in yards specializing in pleasure craft, there have, on the other hand, been introduced a multitude of labor-saving hand-driven and power-driven machines. Today, one no longer sees the fisherman, the boatbuilder, the shipwright, and the master of the yard working side by side in the yard. Production now requires bigger investments and a more clear-cut division of labor, so that the master of the yard will be able to make the payments for the materials for the current job as well as the next.

Today, it is the price and the size that are the deciding factors as to where the fisherman is going to have his boat built, while in times past it was the special boat types offered by different masters that was of overriding importance in the selection of the particular boatyard. The various fishing boats have since World War I become more and more uniform, and on account of the standardized drawings and the uniform requirements, the master shipwrights have found it increasingly difficult to put their personal stamp on their boats; similarly, the local stamp, so evident in the older boats, has been slowly wiped out. The shipwrights of today need only to follow the drawings of the designer and the requirements of the Ships Inspectorate, and this makes the craftsmen ever more specialized and dependent on others. When one doesn't face new requirements and problems, one doesn't need the knowledge and skill of a craftsman; today, there are but few boatbuilders who with nothing but the beach as a yard are able to lay a keel when requested by a fisherman, "Build me a herring boat!"

Timbers are being cut with a pit saw. The timbers are placed underneath the three-legged crane that is used to hoist the logs up on the trestles. Foreground: a wagon used to transport logs. Section of a drawing from Nordby on the island of Fanø by Sexton Th. Schmidt, 1896.

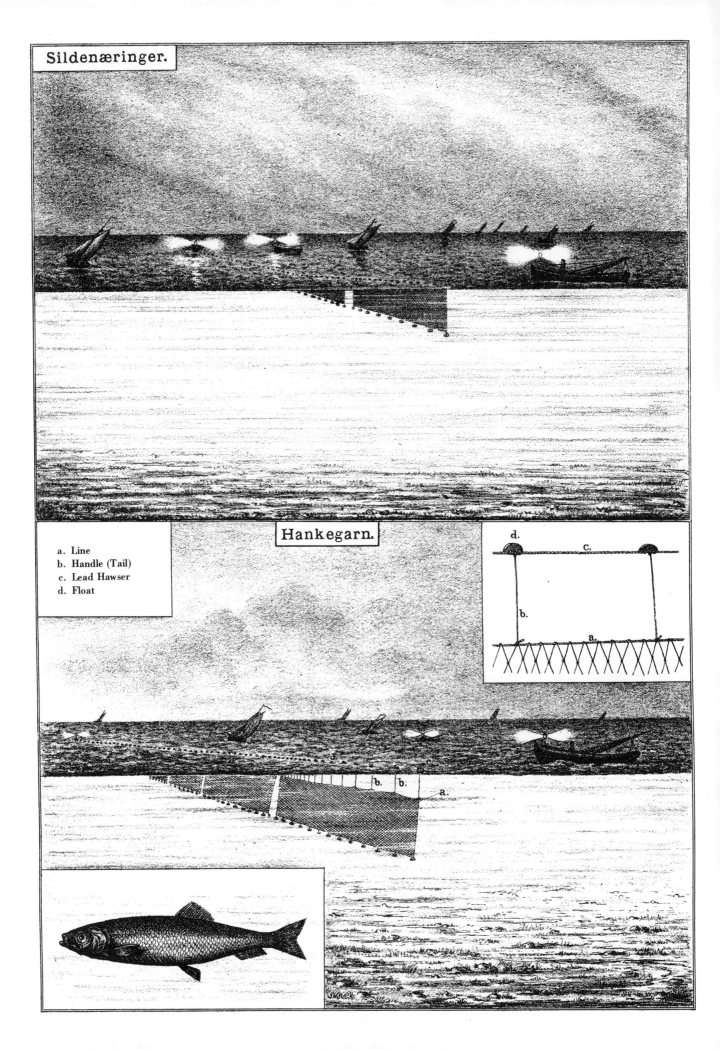

Sildenæringer.

Hankegarn.

a. Line
b. Handle (Tail)
c. Lead Hawser
d. Float

I.
HERRING BOATS

THE HERRING IS WRITTEN ABOUT IN THE OLD SOURCES
more often than any other kind of fish, and it is probably the first type
of fish to have influenced the design of fishing vessels used.

The Boats

Even though the herring fisheries were conducted from a great number
of localities along almost the entire Danish coastline, and the special herring boats varied somewhat in shape, size, and use, they all, with one exception, belonged to the same family of vessels. For the Sound boat, the
Kattegat boat, the Kerteminde boat, and the Bornholm boat were keel-
built vessels with sharp sterns and S-shaped body plans. The older type,
like *Hejmdal*, used in the Great and Little Belts, had a flat stern but its
lines from the third rib forward were not very different from those of its
sharp-sterned sisters. The Sound and Kattegat boats were, as a rule,
lighter than the Belt boats, since they were frequently used in conjunction with set nets, whose tending required boats that didn't labor heavily in the sea, which a heavy boat is apt to do. The Belt, Sound, and
Kattegat boats were also used in the summertime to transport rocks and
gravel. For vessels that normally would be engaged in the easier task of
herring fishing, this was a very heavy type of alternative use. To coun-
teract the extra wear and tear, the fishermen were therefore obliged to
place extra planks on the gunwale and the deck so that the herring nets
would not later get ripped and torn.

When fisheries consultant C. F. Drechsel in 1890 published his book *Oversigt over vore
Saltvandsfiskerier* (*Survey of Our Salt Water Fisheries*) he had able and creative ship-
builders submit drawings of improved fishing vessels to be printed in the book. He also
persuaded fisheries inspector C. Holstein to have several plates included, showing the
best and most common fishing tackle and methods. These technical drawings have been
executed so ably that we today through the instructive details and without any complicated text get a very good idea of the technique of each type of fishery.

The illustrations on the opposite page have been taken from Drechsel's book and
show fishing with two kinds of nets: one, the smaller one at the top, is placed from the
surface down, while the other type of net is placed just below the water's surface.

Opposite:
Top: Herring Fisheries
Bottom: Nets with Handles

An old fisherman and his wife removing the herring from the nets, after the boat has reached harbor. On the left, a half-filled crate of herrings, with the place-name Kerteminde.

The Fisheries

In the Great Belt the fishermen would mostly use special nets, which were positioned about a yard below the water's surface and had handles tied to the messenger rope, one end of which was made fast to the vessel. They fished with these drift nets from sunset until early morning, at which time they were taken on board by two men who pulled in the messenger rope and the lead line, respectively. Another type of net (*nœring*) whose upper part sat flush with the water's surface was, at the end of a drift, pulled on board on a wooden roller, which in the Sound boat was placed forward along the gunwale.

Sales and Markets

The herring that was caught in spring was sent for the most part to Germany and other central European countries. The herring was salted or kept frozen in crates containing chopped ice. From the Great Belt the herring was shipped by mail steamer from Korsør to Kiel. A great deal of the catch from other places along the coast was mainly sold to the local farmers and to smokehouses, as well as to merchants in Copenhagen.

The spring herring is much smaller and skinnier than the fall herring, and it didn't for that reason fetch as high prices. The fall herring fisheries, conducted from August to October, were therefore almost always of greater importance than the spring fisheries. The prices for the Danish herring, however, were always depressed by the Swedish herring, which was caught throughout the winter among the islets and skerries outside the province of Bohuslän.

The Nordenhuse Boat
Hejmdal

The *Hejmdal* of Nyborg was built at Nordenhuse in 1870. Measurement Project No. 16.

Length: 25 ft   5 in. = 7.98 m
Beam: 8 ft 10 in. = 2.77 m
Height: 4 ft   9 in. = 1.49 m
Draft: 4 ft   0 in. = 1.26 m

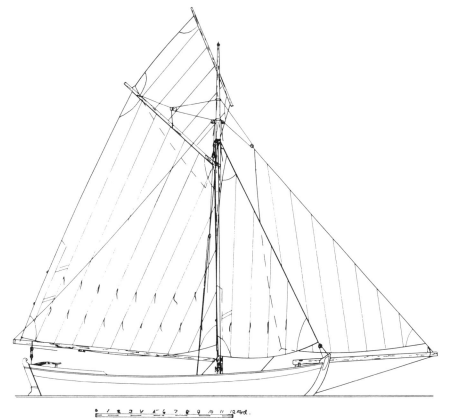

(fod = foot or feet)

Around the turn of the century one could see throughout the southern part of the Great Belt older herring boats like *Hejmdal*, with heart-shaped sterns.

 Hejmdal has a very strong backbone construction, but is otherwise trimly built, and is fastened throughout with treenails, in the overlapping planks as well as the ribs. The vessel's greatest width is exactly in the area of the mast. With its high rudder and steeply sloping leech in the mainsail, it is a type that one would rarely encounter after World

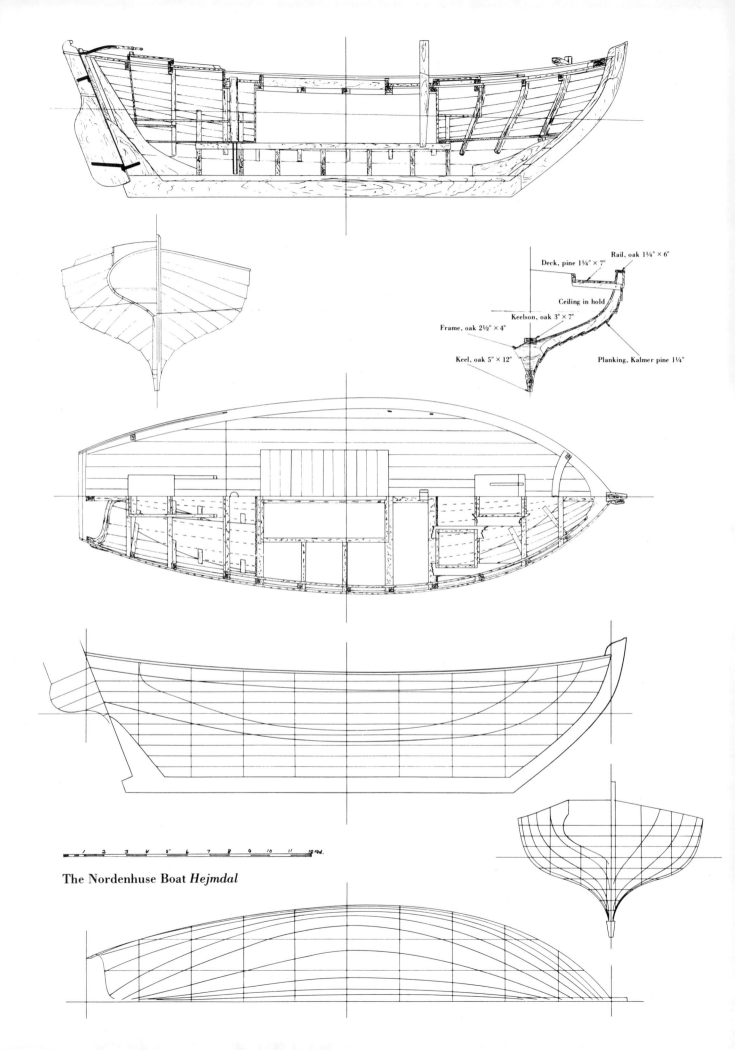

Deck, pine 1¼" × 7"

Rail, oak 1¼" × 6"

Ceiling in hold

Keelson, oak 3" × 7"

Frame, oak 2½" × 4"

Planking, Kalmer pine 1¼"

Keel, oak 5" × 12"

The Nordenhuse Boat *Hejmdal*

War I. The boat, with its ornamented stern, was coated with tar, and the sheer strake was painted green with a white border. Hatches, covers, and the gunwales were painted gray, and the bottom was covered with black tar. Thus, both as a fishing vessel and a cargo vessel, *Hejmdal* looked very picturesque.

Most of the herring boats of this type were built during the winter at the home of the fisherman by a local boatbuilder. The fisherman obtained wood in the forest and, aided by his neighbors, took a hand in the construction of the vessel. The fisherman and the boatbuilder each would have a small farm in addition to their chief occupation, and they were thus well supplied with potatoes and the most common vegetables.

When they fished with herring nets, the crew would consist of three men, who could get some sleep underneath the afterdeck when off watch. They would always retire with all their clothes on in order to be ready if the wind freshened and the nets had to be taken in.

Scene from Troense. Several spritsail boats and a sloop are moored in the harbor. On the right, a square-sterned Belt boat at anchor by the pole. Drawing by Tom Petersen, 1888, in *Danmark* by M. Galschiøt.

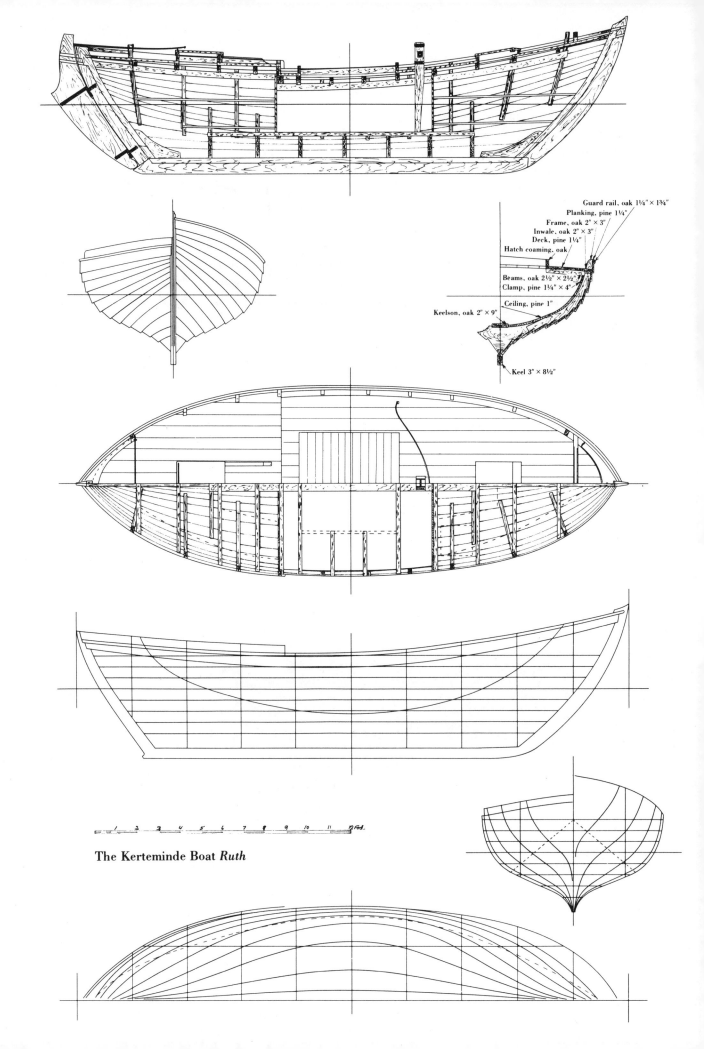

Guard rail, oak 1¼″ × 1¾″
Planking, pine 1¼″
Frame, oak 2″ × 3″
Inwale, oak 2″ × 3″
Deck, pine 1¼″
Hatch coaming, oak
Beams, oak 2½″ × 2½″
Clamp, pine 1¼″ × 4″
Ceiling, pine 1″
Keelson, oak 2″ × 9″
Keel 3″ × 8½″

/ 2 3 4 5 6 7 8 9 10 11 12 Fed.

The Kerteminde Boat *Ruth*

The Kerteminde Boat
Ruth

This boat from Kerteminde was built in 1878. Measurement Project
No. 17.
Length: 25 ft 9 in. = 8.08 m
Beam: 8 ft 5 in. = 2.64 m
Height: 4 ft 3 in. = 1.33 m
Draft: 3 ft 0 in. = 0.94 m

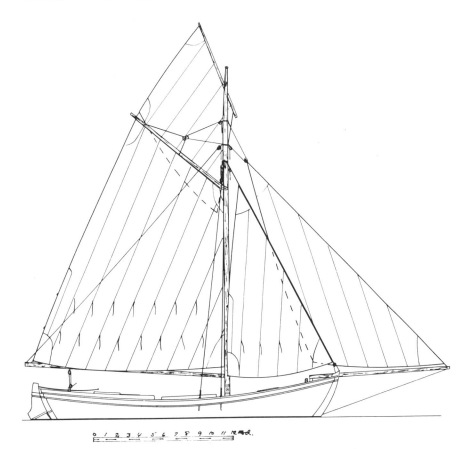

Ruth is a so-called Kerteminde boat. It was used for the same purposes
and during approximately the same time period as *Hejmdal*. But in con-
tradistinction to the latter, it is sharp sterned, like the herring boats
from Bornholm, with which it has many features in common. The rigging and the colors of the deck and the hull are almost identical to those
of the *Hejmdal*.

Ruth was employed in the herring and mackerel fisheries, its crew consisting of two men and a boy. During the fall fisheries, boats would often arrive from the islands off the southern part of Fyn and Sjælland, their owners wanting to join the fishermen from the shores of the Great Belt.

Herring boats outside Kerteminde harbor about 1905. The boat in the foreground—which was never given any name—was one of the few boats in this area painted white. The sides of other boats of this type were tarred black.

THE SOUND BOATS

DURING THE LAST CENTURY MANY OF THE FISHERMEN
from the shores of the Sound would catch shrimp during the season in
the waters off Swedish Småland and also north of the island of Ærø.
With their fast and light boats they would carry the catch to Masned-
sund and even all the way to Copenhagen, where they would have an
opportunity to say hello to their families before setting out on the next
trip.

Many fishermen in the Småland Sea, in the southern part of the Great
Belt, and off the islands south of Fyn were impressed by the neat, swift,
and easily maneuverable Sound boats, and down through the years
many boats of the type represented by *Thora* were purchased by fishermen in these areas to be used in the herring fisheries. In the same
period, a great number of Kattegat herring boats, like *Maries Minde*,
were also purchased for fishing in these southern waters.

In principle, the Sound and Kattegat boats were of the same type as
the Belt boats and were built with the same fisheries in mind, but they
were lighter and neater and, in addition, had floor timbers and futtocks

Two Kattegat boats leaving the harbor on the island of Anholt, powered by their motors
and with the mainsails up. The one in the foreground is *Alfa*, built at Gilleleje in 1903. H
201 is the half-decked boat *Haabet* of Gilleleje and built at Viken in Scania in 1888. The
vessels were equipped with motors of seven and four horsepower, respectively. *Haabet*
is now owned by the Danish National Museum. Photograph from 1907.

The Kattegat boat *Oskar* was built in Viken (Scania) for a fisherman at Gilleleje in 1903. *Oskar* was more or less of the same type and dimensions as *Maries Minde*. Two men in a small boat are painting the topsides. In the background is seen a ketch being careened, and to the right is a gaff-rigged half-decked boat.

treenailed together, which contrasts with the Belt boats, where these parts of the boat were staggered. Some boatbuilders were of the opinion that the framework of the Belt boats ought to be more flexible, but they would in that case be more vulnerable when they became old and worn. Both kinds of framework represent local methods and styles of construction frequently used in small boats.

Fishing for herring at Kerteminde. Some of the boats can be seen pulling in their nets, while others already have their catch on board and are sailing home. The masts on the boats with lanterns have been taken down so that the pitching will be at a minimum. At the upper left can be seen a square-sterned herring boat, among all the sharp-sterned Belt boats. Woodcut by Karel Sedivy in *Illustreret Tidende*.

The Sound Boat
Thora

The *Thora* was built at Skovshoved in 1913. Measurement Project
No. 6.
Length: 24 ft   0 in. = 7.53 m
Beam: 8 ft   9 in. = 2.75 m
Height: 3 ft 10 in. = 1.20 m
Draft: ca. 3 ft   6 in. = 1.10 m

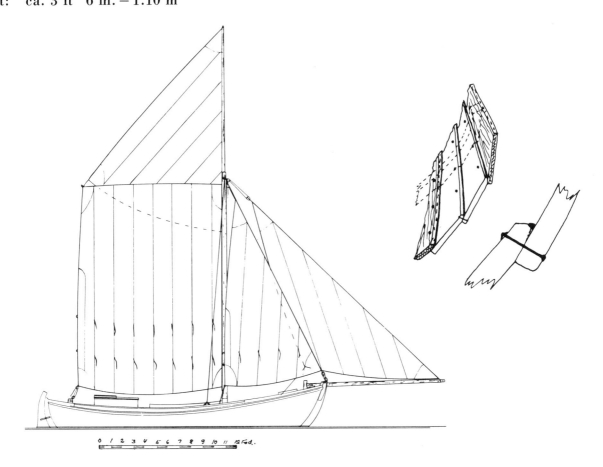

Thora is a typical representative of the spritsail-rigged, lightly built
Sound boats. Compared with other herring boats, this vessel has a small
carrying capacity with very sharp lines in the forebody. The fishermen
of the Sound are of the opinion that it is necessary for a boat to have a
sharp bow in order to get through the choppy waves so often experienced in the Sound.

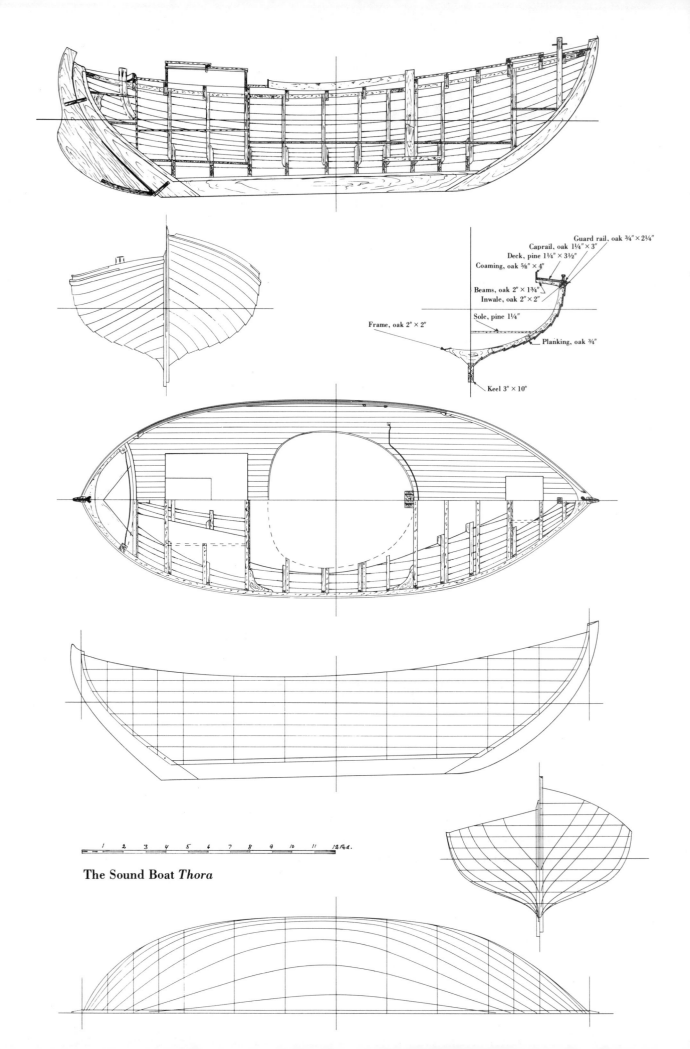

Guard rail, oak ¾" × 2¼"

Caprail, oak 1¼" × 3"

Deck, pine 1¼" × 3½"

Coaming, oak ⅝" × 4"

Beams, oak 2" × 1¾"

Inwale, oak 2" × 2"

Frame, oak 2" × 2"

Sole, pine 1¼"

Planking, oak ¾"

Keel 3" × 10"

1 2 3 4 5 6 7 8 9 10 11 12 Fod.

The Sound Boat *Thora*

This type of boat is used along the Sound, from Copenhagen north to Helsingør. But the older vessels were a bit more full-built than *Thora* and her successors. Following the introduction of the internal-combustion engine, the boats were supplied with a well, in addition to a poop aft and a cabin, with a pair of bunks, forward. The bulwark was also at that time made a little higher. Like so many other vessels, *Thora* was rebuilt along these general lines, in 1916.

Thora was used for fishing with traps and plain angling but mostly for fishing for herring with nets. A crew of two or three men would share the proceeds. Each man would set his own nets and give over a certain part of his catch to the boat, either in the form of cash or fresh fish. The owner would use the boat's share to pay for new equipment, repairs, and upkeep. When the boat was employed in fishing with traps or hooks and lines, the crew would be paid by the owner for their work.

Herring boats in the harbor of Tårbæk. The boats are all equipped with motors. The fishermen are putting their gear in order following a night of fishing. On the decks are seen lines, floats, and buoys. The vessels' sprits are placed along the gunwale. Photo from *Dansk Saltvandsfiskeri*, 1935.

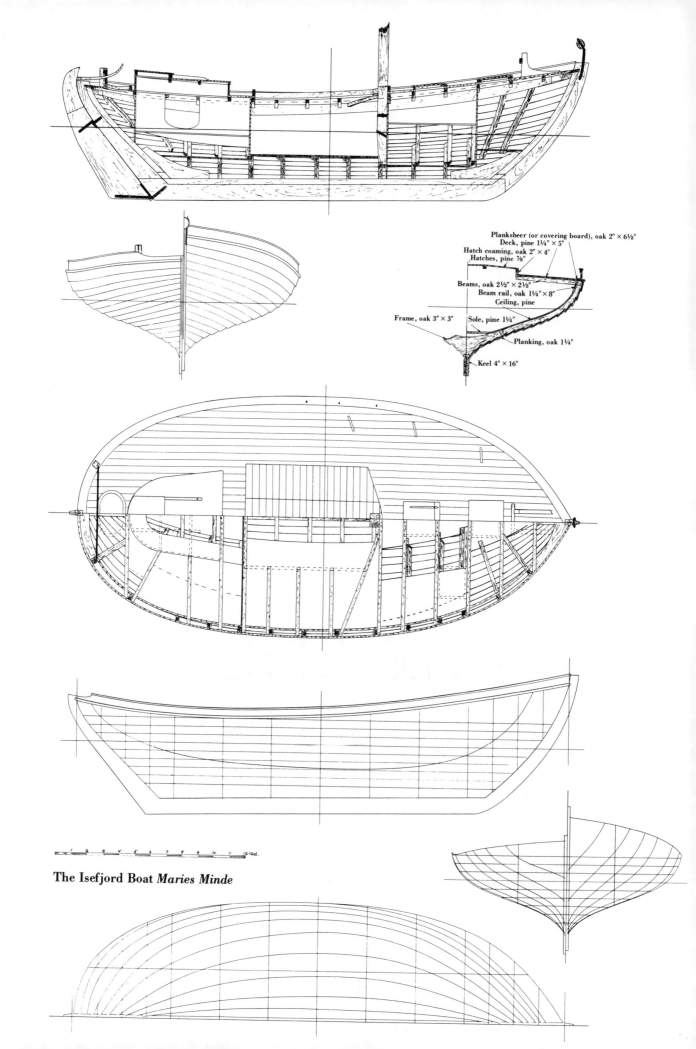

Planksheer (or covering board), oak 2″ × 6½″
Deck, pine 1¼″ × 5″
Hatch coaming, oak 2″ × 4″
Hatches, pine ⅞″

Beams, oak 2½″ × 2½″
Beam rail, oak 1¼″ × 8″
Ceiling, pine

Frame, oak 3″ × 3″   Sole, pine 1¼″

Planking, oak 1¼″

Keel 4″ × 16″

The Isefjord Boat _Maries Minde_

The Isefjord Boat
Maries Minde

The Isefjord boat *Maries Minde* of Hundested was built at Liseleje in
1895. Measurement Project No. 4.

Length: 31 ft   0 in. = 9.73 m
Beam: 14 ft   4 in. = 4.50 m
Height: 4 ft 10 in. = 1.52 m
Draft: ca. 4 ft   6 in. = 1.41 m

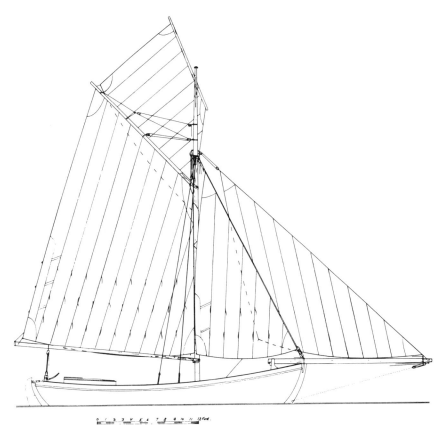

Most of the representatives of this solid and lightly constructed shoal-
draft boat were built at Lynæs, Hundested, or Liseleje. In contradis-
tinction to the Sound boats, they were very wide in relation to their
length and had fuller bows above the water. Their great width, however, didn't reduce their seaworthiness in the rough Kattegat; on the
contrary, it made the boats more maneuverable when the nets were to be
set.

Like all the Isefjord boats, *Maries Minde* has firm bulwarks on the planksheer in both bows; the bulwark in the middle has been bolted with angle irons.

This type of boat was almost exclusively used to fish herring with nets and to carry potatoes to Copenhagen. Many boats were ordered by fishermen in Denmark's more southerly waters and in the Vejle area, where they were used to carry rocks and gravel. When motors were introduced, many of these boats were made longer by four to six feet, and provision was made for an engine well, so that they could be used to fish with an otter trawl. *Maries Minde* in 1905 was furnished with a Rap motor from Aalborg with a specially rigged outboard propeller, and later on, a well was constructed inside the boat.

Fjord boats beating to windward outside Spodsbjerg. The drawing shows clearly the balance and buoyancy of the broad fjord and Kattegat boats. Pen-and-ink sketch by Thorolf Pedersen in M. Galschiøt: *Danmark*, 1891.

THE BORNHOLM BOATS

DURING THE YEARS 1870 TO 1900, THE SOUND AND THE KAT-tegat boats as well as the Belt boats were used at the same time in the waters off Småland and in the Great Belt. From these boats they would mainly fish herring with nets with handles, and in the summertime between the fishing seasons the boats sailed as cargo boats with rocks and gravel for the highways, since rocks from the sea bottom were more durable than rocks quarried on land.

The harbor of Listed on the island of Bornholm in the early 1900s. On the left are seen a few herring boats (similar to *Haabet*); in the center is an older type; and on the right can be seen a part of a sharp-sterned open boat. In the background one can make out a few small ketches, probably used to transport sandstone.

Around the turn of the century, the herring fishermen of Bornholm started to fish off Småland and in the western part of the Baltic. The herring fisheries off Bornholm came later in the year than the fishing season in the Belts, since the herring in the Danish waters moved farther east in the fall; thus, the Bornholmers found out that they could enjoy two big herring fisheries in autumn, if they sailed their small boats at an early date to the southern Danish waters. In addition, it was easy to sell the fish, since there were interested buyers in Stubbekøbing and other places.

Since the boats from Bornholm, even with their small size, were superior to the Belt and Sound boats as far as seaworthiness was concerned, the local fishermen in the Langeland Belt became interested in this type, and in the period down to 1920 a considerable number of Bornholm boats were sold to them. Thus, until World War I, one could see both Sound and Kattegat boats, Belt boats and Bornholm boats, such as *Haabet* of Listed, in the same area and catching the same kind of fish. They were all sharp-sterned shoal-draft vessels; as far as their construction was concerned, they must be said to belong to the same group, but their local features indicated that they had been built in different places in Denmark.

Bornholm herring boats with tanned sails. The boat to the far left is spritsail-rigged. The boat on the right has left port with the aid of both sails and oars. The Bornholm fishermen always had oars as part of their equipment, since this was required by their insurers.

The Bornholm Boat
Haabet

The *Haabet* of Listed was built at Svaneke in 1900. Measurement Project No. 43.

Length: 25 ft   0 in. = 7.85 m
Beam: 9 ft   2 in. = 2.88 m
Height: 3 ft 10 in. = 1.20 m
Draft: ca. 3 ft   6 in. = 1.10 m

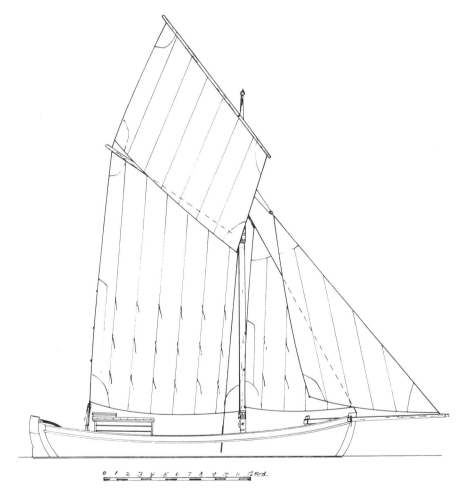
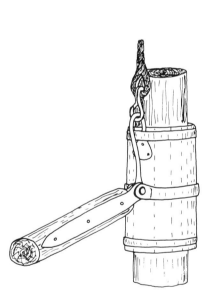

Haabet is a strong and solidly built vessel with full entrance. Like almost all Bornholm boats, it has been treenailed through planking and ribs, between which oil paper has been inserted in order to prevent the spreading of dry rot.

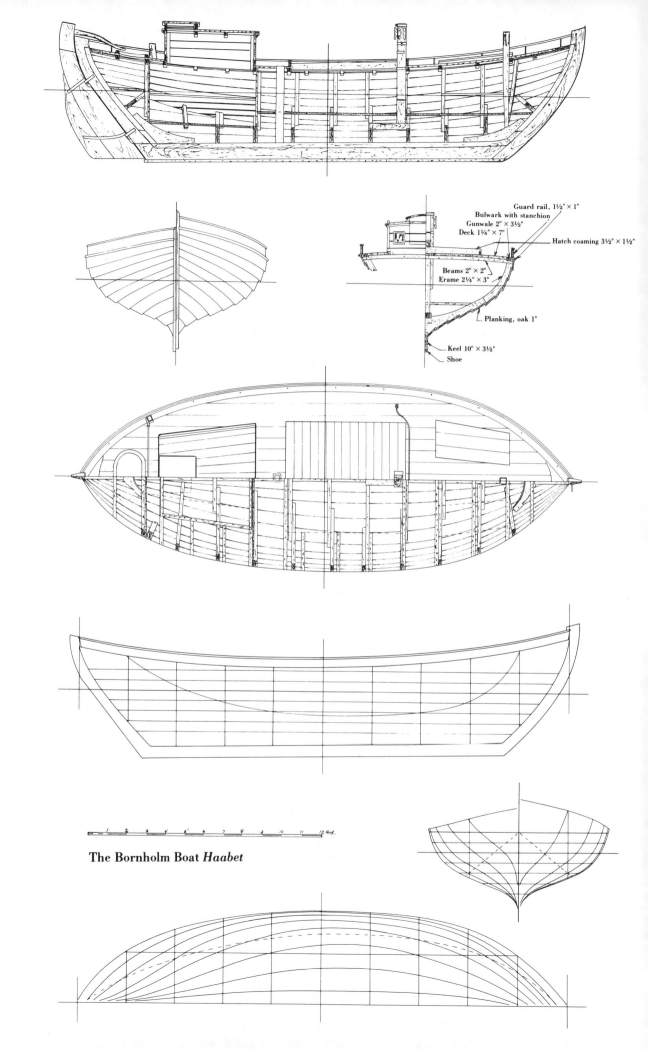

Guard rail, 1½" × 1"
Bulwark with stanchion
Gunwale 2" × 3½"
Deck 1¼" × 7"
Hatch coaming 3½" × 1½"
Beams 2" × 2"
Frame 2¼" × 3"
Planking, oak 1"
Keel 10" × 3½"
Shoe

The Bornholm Boat *Haabet*

Haabet was used to fish salmon and to jig for cod, but was in the main used in the herring fisheries with nets that resemble the nets with handles in the Great Belt. When the nets are pulled in, they are bunched together by the gunwale and are brought on board from the forward hatch in a large bundle. A great part of the Bornholm herring was exported in a smoked or salted condition.

The crew usually consisted of three or four men, and the fisherman who owned the boat didn't, as a rule, own the equipment, since each fisherman brought his own nets and lines.

The fishermen used to call boats like *Haabet* "the round-bowed" (*rundstævnede*) type.

A boat from Bornholm used to fish salmon, from around 1900. The vessel had sharp ends, and the high peak of the topsail yard is also a feature that was retained on Bornholm boats throughout the age of sail.

THE ACCEPTANCE OF THE MOTOR

AFTER THE BOATS OF THE BORNHOLMERS HAD GAINED AC-
ceptance in the Great Belt, the boatbuilders at Lohals also began to
build vessels with many of the characteristics of the Bornholm boats.
These boats, of the same type as *Victoria* of Lohals, were mostly to fish
with otter trawls in the Baltic and the Great Belt, as a result of the introduction of the motor. Nyborg boats, such as *Helga* of Omø, were also
developed at this time and were used in the same fisheries as the Lohals
boats; however, they were much more modest in appearance and construction and were also much less expensive. With their bigger engines,
tonnage, and intensively conducted otter trawling, these two types took
the place of the old sharp-sterned and other similar herring boats.
These are still the types that characterize the Danish fisheries in the
inner waters. The only difference is that the planking, instead of being
lapstrake (clinker), has been superseded by carvel construction and the
motors are bigger.

Motors were installed in some fishing boats as early as the 1880s. The
earliest motors were not intended to be a means of propulsion but only
to aid in pulling in the trawls. But the fishermen soon had the motor
drive a propeller that was placed below the water's surface but connected with an ingenious contraption attached to the gunwale in the

The deck of a Danish seiner, with windlass, hatches, etc. 1929.

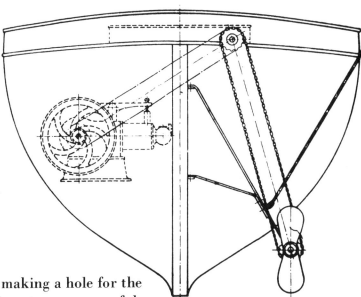

The first ship's motors were installed for the sole purpose of pulling the seines up on the rollers. But it was soon found that with a chain drive the motor could be connected with a propeller, which was attached to an iron frame bolted to the stern as well as a stanchion outside the engine room. Drawing from Houmøller's Workshop in Frederikshavn, 1899.

rear. They had been afraid to weaken the stern by making a hole for the propeller's shaft, but it was tried and the experiment was successful, and the so-called bicycle propeller was abandoned with no regrets. In the year 1900 there were already many factories that advertised ship motors in the membership publication of the Society of Danish Fishermen, and motors were added to a great number of fishing boats during the following decade. As most boats began to be equipped with motors, the lines of the sterns were made fuller in order to be able to carry the increased weight. Even with the first inboard motors, the main purpose was to haul in seines and otter trawls, and second to add a few knots to the vessel's speed in good weather. Topsails and jibs became an increasingly rare sight even then, and when the engines increased in size and power, these sails disappeared completely, and the rig was used principally as an aid when trawls were to be hauled in. The rig was also held in reserve for when the motor broke down, this being a rather frequent occurrence in the beginning.

Even today, these fishing boats are equipped with sails, but they are smaller than those of *Victoria* and *Helga* and are only used in rough weather.

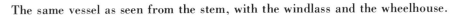

The same vessel as seen from the stem, with the windlass and the wheelhouse.

◆ 35

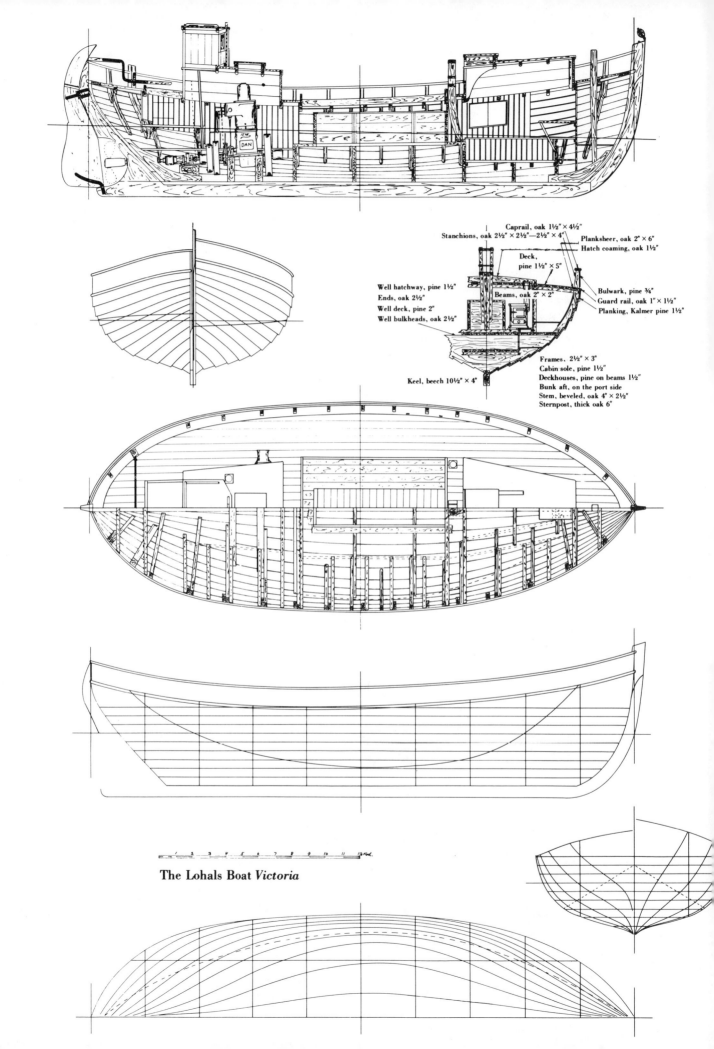

Caprail, oak 1½″ × 4½″
Stanchions, oak 2½″ × 2½″—2½″ × 4″
Planksheer, oak 2″ × 6″
Hatch coaming, oak 1½″
Deck, pine 1½″ × 5″
Well hatchway, pine 1½″
Ends, oak 2½″
Well deck, pine 2″
Well bulkheads, oak 2½″
Beams, oak 2″ × 2″
Bulwark, pine ¾″
Guard rail, oak 1″ × 1½″
Planking, Kalmer pine 1½″

Keel, beech 10½″ × 4″

Frames, 2½″ × 3″
Cabin sole, pine 1½″
Deckhouses, pine on beams 1½″
Bunk aft, on the port side
Stem, beveled, oak 4″ × 2½″
Sternpost, thick oak 6″

The Lohals Boat _Victoria_

The Lohals Boat
Victoria

This boat was built at Lohals in 1918. Measurement Project No. 20.

Length: 32 ft 5 in. = 10.17 m
Beam: 11 ft 9 in. = 3.69 m
Height: 4 ft 6 in. = 1.41 m
Draft: ca. 4 ft 0 in. = 1.26 m

Victoria is a strong and robust vessel, furnished originally with a motor and carrying only a mainsail and jib. As with most of the other Lohals boats, whose length was between 25 and 33 feet, its stem above water is almost vertical. *Victoria* was chiefly engaged in the otter trawl and herring fisheries in the western part of the Baltic Sea. A crew of two was all that was needed when fishing with seine nets, whereas there were three men on board when they fished for herring.

Victoria pulled up on the slipway in the harbor of Lohals. In this picture one can see that the bulwark has been made higher, and the wheelhouse has been enlarged. One can clearly see the seine rollers aft.

Helga outside an old warehouse at the harbor of Fejø. The eel seine has been set across the boom to dry. Photograph from 1964.

The Nyborg Boat
Helga

The *Helga* of Omø was built at Nyborg in 1913. Measurement Project
No. 19.

Length: 27 ft 9 in. = 8.71 m
Beam: 10 ft 11 in. = 3.43 m
Height: 4 ft 6 in. = 1.41 m
Draft: ca. 4 ft 6 in. = 1.41 m

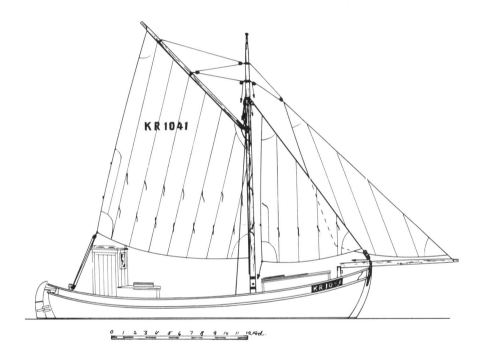

Helga is a typical otter trawler from the inner Danish waters. It features a rather wider covering board, which provides the vessel with its main strength. With its large well and rather sharp ends, it can be used in all kinds of fisheries. It is an inexpensive and seaworthy craft which during the interwar period was introduced into the Kattegat, the Baltic, the Sound, and the Belts.

More than a third of the cubic content of the vessel is devoted to space for the engine. On the fishing boats of the present day, ever greater space is given over to the motor, while the masts have become shorter and the wheelhouses have become bigger.

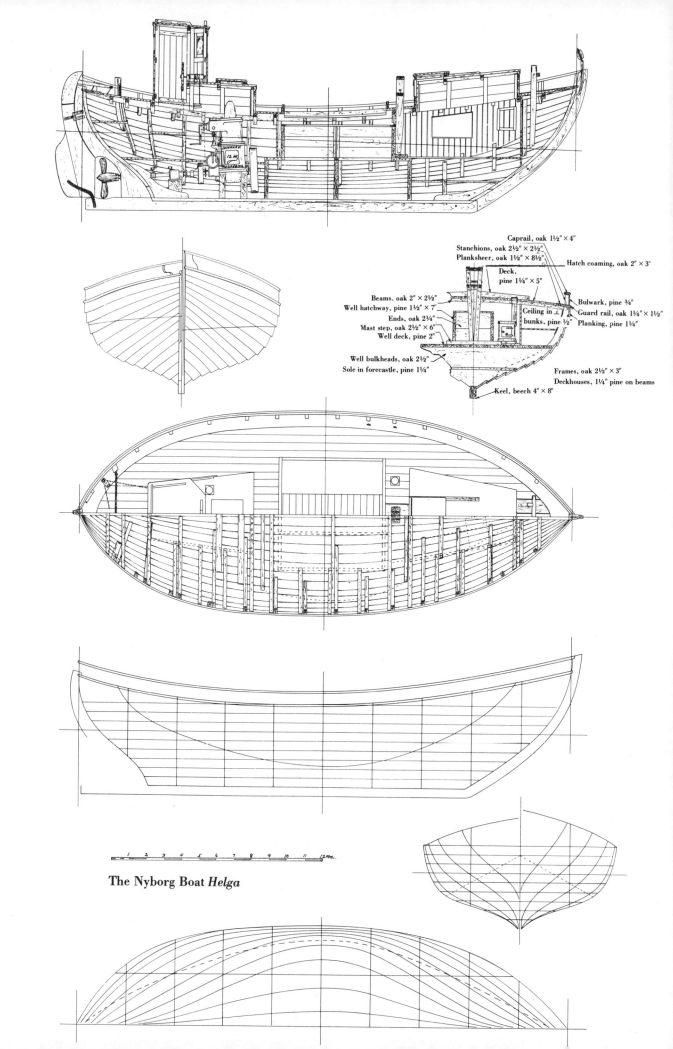

Caprail, oak 1½" × 4"
Stanchions, oak 2½" × 2½"
Planksheer, oak 1½" × 8½"
Hatch coaming, oak 2" × 3"
Deck, pine 1¼" × 5"
Beams. oak 2" × 2½"
Well hatchway, pine 1½" × 7"
Ends, oak 2¼"
Mast step, oak 2½" × 6"
Well deck, pine 2"
Well bulkheads, oak 2½"
Sole in forecastle, pine 1¼"
Bulwark, pine ¾"
Guard rail, oak 1¼" × 1½"
Ceiling in bunks, pine ½"
Planking, pine 1¼"
Frames, oak 2½" × 3"
Deckhouses, 1¼" pine on beams
Keel, beech 4" × 8"

The Nyborg Boat *Helga*

1 2 3 4 5 6 7 8 9 10 11 12 Fod.

THE FORMATION OF FISHERMEN'S ORGANIZATIONS

IN THE SECOND DECADE OF THIS CENTURY THE NYBORG AND Lohals boats became popular in the areas from where boats had previously been exported to the Great Belt. They were also introduced in the Sound, where, together with the now-motorized Skovshoved boats, they took over in some of the fisheries, among them the herring fisheries, that previously had been carried out along the coast in small open boats, such as the Snekkersten boat. These boats were supplied with motors and were used to tend pound nets and traps, a type of fishery in which they are still engaged.

Off the island of Bornholm, and prior to the introduction of decked boats, the fishermen used open boats like *Odin* and *Jens* exclusively and fished for herring all through the year. The fishery was carried out from flat-sterned or sharp-sterned vessels that were called *eger*. Very seaworthy vessels, they were also used by Swedish fishermen who had them built on Bornholm. During the years after 1900 these boats were superseded by decked boats like *Haabet*, which continued to be built on the island down to the year 1940. No carvel-built vessel was supposed to have been constructed on Bornholm before that time, but during and after World War II they began to build twenty-ton standard fishing vessels. At the end of the 1920s six or seven families from Lohals who moved from the island of Langeland to Tejn and took their Lohals boats with them found that they were very well suited to the new fishing environment. But the Lohals boats did not create any demand for similar boats among the Bornholm fishermen.

At the time that the decked boats were introduced and became popular, a strong organization was formed among the fishermen. They were forced to borrow money from the banks in order to obtain the new boats, but created only a limited liability for each by having three or four men share the ownership of a boat. The bank also demanded that the boats on which loans had been taken out should be insured, and the fishermen collectively took out a policy with an insurance company through their new society.

Two Sound boats pulled up on shore at Humlebæk. Next to the dinghies is a wheelbarrow for the fishing gear. Washed pencil drawing by Christian Blache.

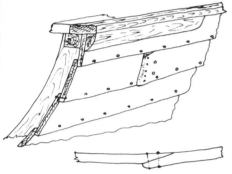

In the 1930s the Bornholm fishermen had a very strong organization, a fact that was made evident by the way they allocated work and profit when the demand for herring was low. When the fish wholesaler in Copenhagen or some other place ordered a certain quantity of fish to be delivered on a certain date, the organization gave each fisherman permission to land only a certain quantity of fish during that particular period. In this way, no fisherman would catch more than could be sold and at the same time it prevented some fishermen from earning a disproportionately greater amount than their fellows. If a fisherman had caught more herring in his nets than he could deliver to the organization, the excess quantity was, as a rule, sold or smoked on the island. This system might well result in a boat going out to fish no more than once a week, but the general opinion was that it was better that some earned less than they otherwise could, if it would prevent other fishermen from suffering.

Odin in Gudhjem harbor, 1970. The mainsail and the staysail are up, and one can clearly see how the topmast is loosely attached to the mainmast.

The Spritsail Boat
from Snekkersten

This type of boat was built at Snekkersten in 1897. Measurement Project No. 78.
Length: 16 ft 6 in. = 5.18 m
Beam: 5 ft 8 in. = 1.78 m
Height: 2 ft 3 in. = 0.70 m
Draft: ca. 2 ft 0 in. = 0.63 m

The Snekkersten boats were all small open boats that were used in conjunction with herring nets, eel traps, fishing with hook and line, and the tending of permanent pound nets, which had been introduced in the Sound in the 1880s.

   The Snekkersten boat was a lightly built craft with a spritsail rig and a fish-shaped mast step. The rudder was carved from a single piece of wood, this being customary in the boats in the Sound. This type of boat did not use a jib when working and was not supplied with any shrouds to brace the mast athwartships, since the builders relied exclusively on the strength of the mast itself.

A small Sound boat in fair weather. The boat carries a spritsail and topsail, but the staysail has been taken down, so that the oarsman forward will have enough space to be able to row. The men are rowing the boat forward in the calm sea, standing and facing forward. Chalk drawing from ca. 1900.

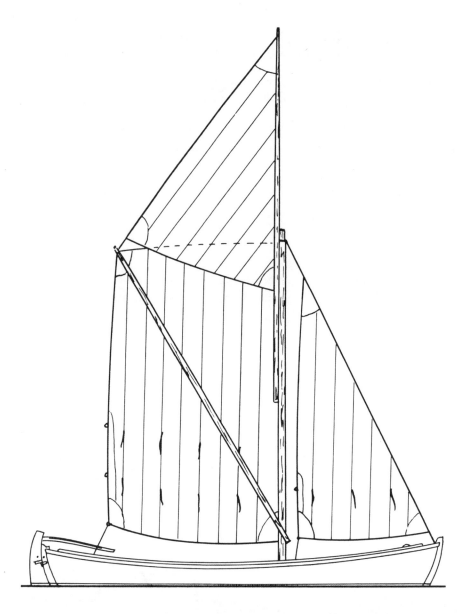

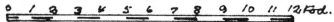

0 1 2 3 4 5 6 7 8 9 10 11 12 Fod.

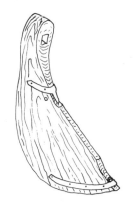

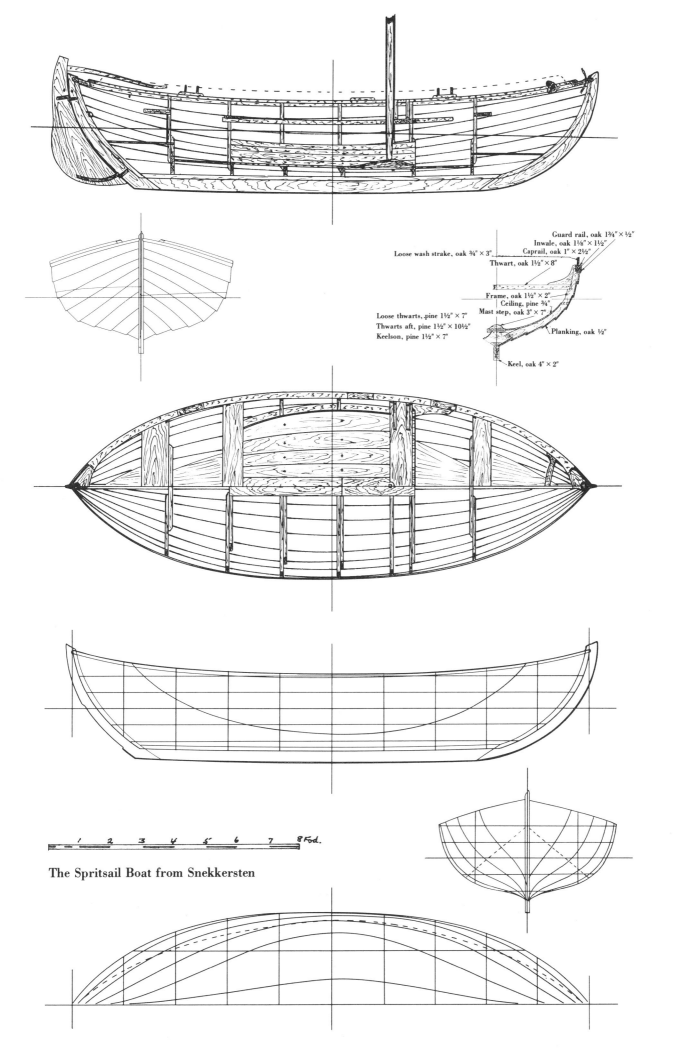

Guard rail, oak 1¾″ × ½″
Inwale, oak 1⅛″ × 1½″
Caprail, oak 1″ × 2½″
Loose wash strake, oak ¾″ × 3″
Thwart, oak 1½″ × 8″

Frame, oak 1½″ × 2″
Ceiling, pine ¾″
Mast step, oak 3″ × 7″

Loose thwarts, .pine 1½″ × 7″
Thwarts aft, pine 1½″ × 10½″
Keelson, pine 1½″ × 7″

Planking, oak ½″

Keel, oak 4″ × 2″

1   2   3   4   5   6   7   8 Fod.

The Spritsail Boat from Snekkersten

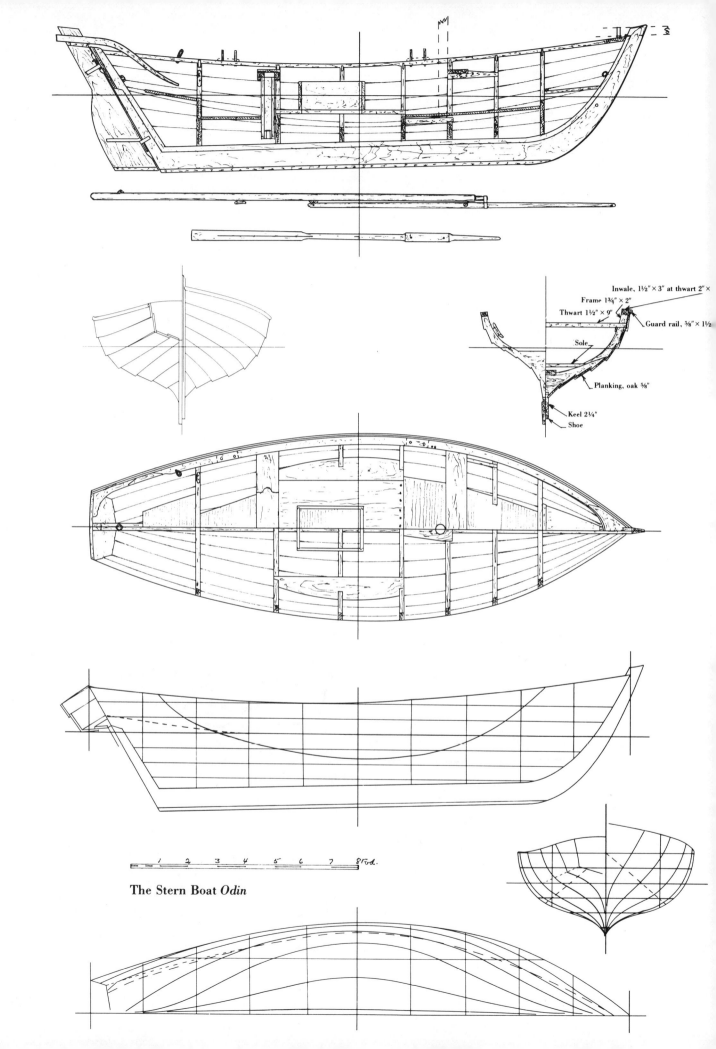

Inwale, 1½" × 3" at thwart 2" ×
Frame 1¾" × 2"
Thwart 1½" × 9"
Guard rail, ⅝" × 1½
Sole
Planking, oak ⅝"
Keel 2¼"
Shoe

1   2   3   4   5   6   7   8 Fod.

The Stern Boat *Odin*

The Stern Boat
Odin

The *Odin* was built at Gudhjem in 1892. Measurement Project No. 37.
Length: 18 ft 9 in. = 5.89 m
Beam: 6 ft 1 in. = 1.91 m
Height: 2 ft 9 in. = 0.86 m
Draft: ca. 2 ft 6 in. = 0.79 m

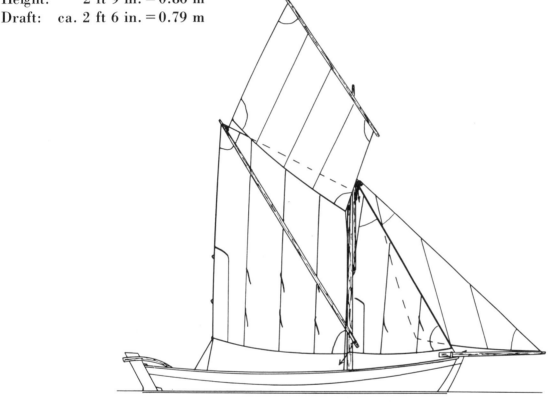

Odin is an older Bornholm type, the lines of which recur in the later
sharp-sterned boats. The plank laps are fastened together with clenched
nails, but joined to the ribs with iron rivets with square heads.

Boats like *Odin*, which normally had a crew of two or three men,
were used in the salmon, herring, and cod fisheries.

During the fishing of herring, the well hatch could be removed by
unscrewing a few tap bolts and replaced with a flat floor, and the few
holes in the well stopped with cork plugs.

Odin departing Gudhjem harbor, ca. 1920. The tanned sails are patched. The curved tiller is clearly visible; it is a common feature of Bornholm's small boats.

A two-masted open boat from Allinge. The sharp ends and the peaked topsail yard are marked characteristics of the Bornholm boats. Pencil drawing by Carl Baagøe, August 1873.

The Double-ended Boat
Jens

This boat was built at Gudhjem ca. 1880. Measurement Project No. 39.
Length: 20 ft 0 in. = 6.28 m
Beam: 7 ft 3 in. = 2.28 m
Height: 3 ft 1 in. = 0.97 m
Draft: ca. 2 ft 6 in. = 0.79 m

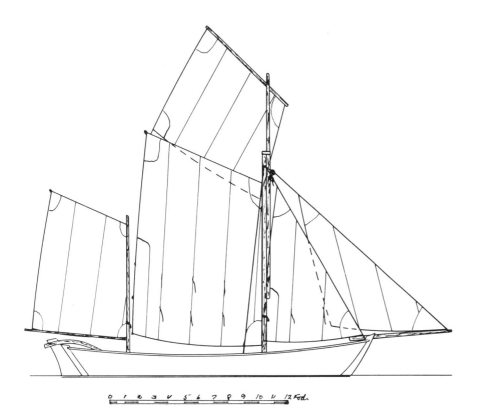

This type of boat, which was used in the salmon and herring fisheries as well as jigging for cod, was called the two-prowed (*tvestævnede*) type by the people of Bornholm.

The oak plank laps are held together with nails forged by hand, and clenched inside the hull.

Boats like *Jens* in time replaced the flat-sterned boats. They all had mainmasts divided into a lower mast and a loose extension.

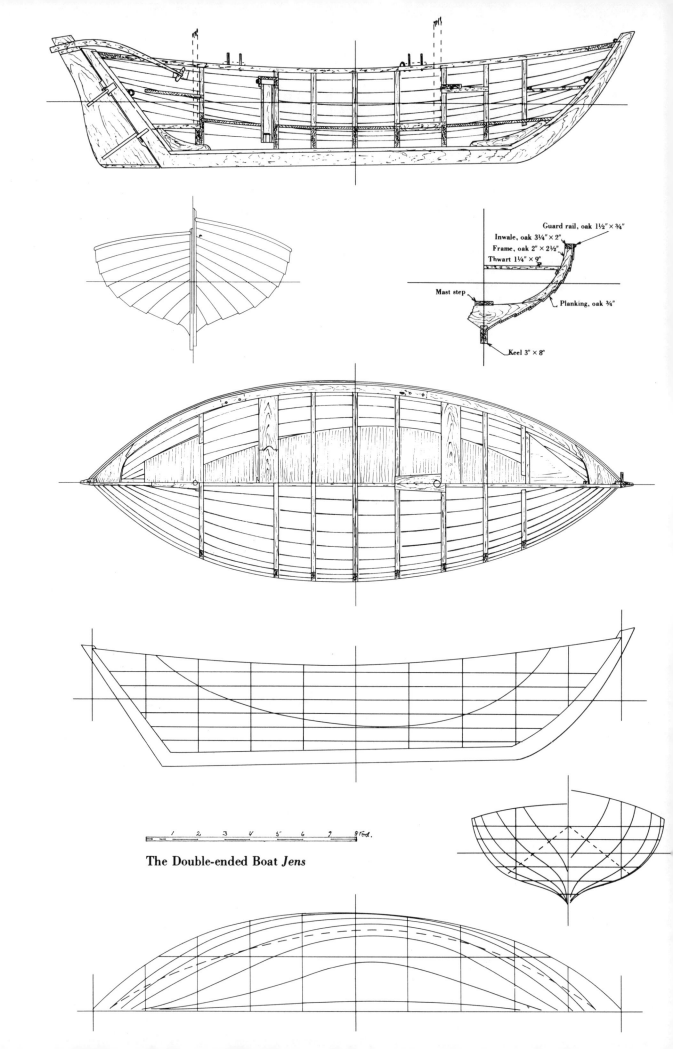

Guard rail, oak 1½" × ¾"

Inwale, oak 3¼" × 2"

Frame, oak 2" × 2½"

Thwart 1¼" × 9"

Mast step

Planking, oak ¾"

Keel 3" × 8"

1 2 3 4 5 6 7 8 Fod.

The Double-ended Boat *Jens*

II.
SPRITSAIL CRAFT

THE SPRITSAIL CRAFT WERE SMALL, OPEN, SHARP-STERNED vessels that were in wide use through the area between Middelfart on the Little Belt south to the islands of Ærø and Femern. These boats were also frequently used as ferries and pilot boats in the waters off the southern part of Sjælland.

The Boats

The name of this type of vessel (in Danish, *smakkejolle*) relates to its type of rig. In the southern Danish waters, a square spritsail was always called *smakke* or *smakkesejl*, and the boats that carried two or three spritsails were called *smakkejoller*. Each sail was hoisted on its own mast, which had been secured through a hole in the thwart but was not supported by shrouds. The advantage in using several small sails and an equal number of masts lay in the fact that the sails could be balanced to conform to the force of the prevailing winds. Thus, steering never became a great problem. For example, on a three-sail boat, if the wind grew stronger, the fishermen would start by taking down the mast

A two-masted spritsail boat moored outside the rest home at Middelfart. The sails and the sprits have been tied to the masts.

and sail aft; if the wind grew even stronger, the forward mast and sail would come down. The main mast and sail would also come down if the weather became very rough, in which case the foremast rig, being smaller, would be put in the midship position.

The boats were always keel- and clinker-built narrow boats, constructed in boatyards along the Great Belt or at Eckernförde, a boat-building center.

The Fisheries

The spritsail boats were mainly used to catch herring and mackerel with a special type of seine. This type of fishing was usually carried out to best advantage where shallow waters merge into the deep sea. The seine was placed in a diagonal position to the current, just where the depth suddenly increased. The shoals (schools) of herring or mackerel would be led by the current diagonally into the net, and the fishermen, in order to speed up this process, would stick a long pole with a barrel-shaped head into the water and with a back-and-forth motion would try to force the fish to swim in the right direction and into the seine. While fishing, the masts would always be down, so that the boat would not roll more than was necessary.

Two spritsail craft in the sound outside Svendborg. The people in the boat in the foreground are probably summer visitors, the men wearing felt hats and the lady a white dress. Drawing by Tom Petersen in M. Galschiøt: *Danmark*, 1887.

This type of fishery, however, kept the men busy only part time—during the fall—and was not sufficient to support a family. The fishermen would consequently have a little farm on the side, and in the summer they would catch some cod with hook and line or flounder or other bottomfish in nets. The herring was sold to local buyers, who fetched it themselves and sold it to the consumers. The cod, however, was sold to other buyers whose larger smacks called at the various fishing grounds.

They used to fish with the help of poles wherever the natural conditions made this method suitable. They poled from open dinghies off Bornholm, with flatners on the Limfjord, and in the Sound with spritsail boats; in the Sound they used stones and rocks instead of poles, throwing them behind the shoal in order to frighten the fish.

This type of fishing came to an end in the interwar period, when otter trawls and bigger motor vessels were introduced. The old spritsail craft were then used to tend pound nets, the main catch being cod, of which there was an unbelievably large number in the 1920s in the waters south of the Danish isles.

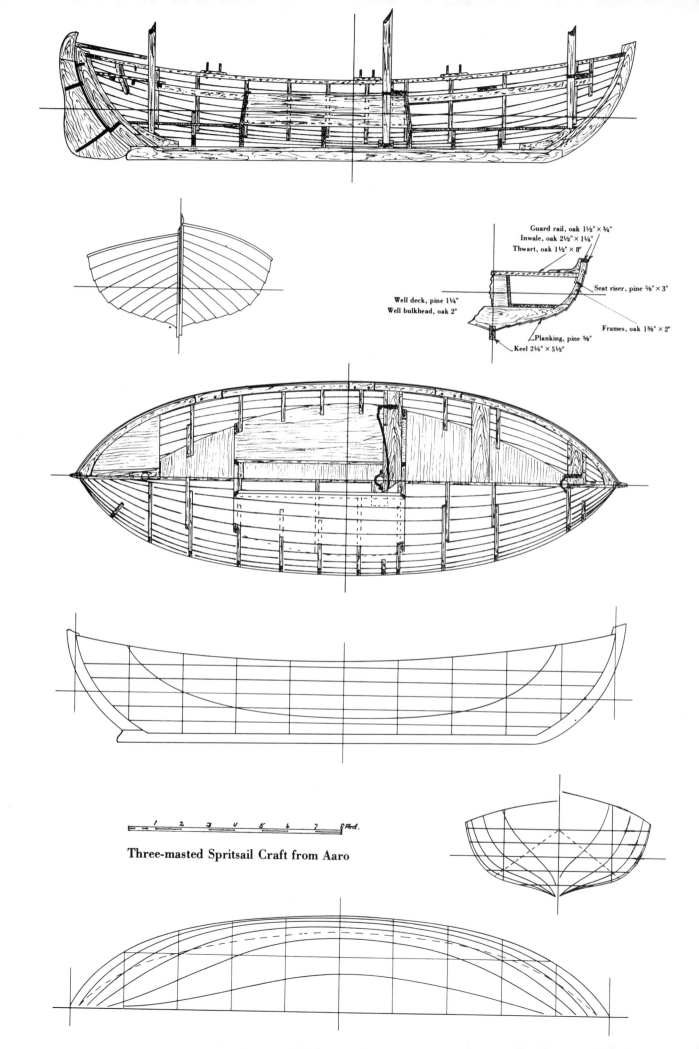

Guard rail, oak 1½" × ¾"
Inwale, oak 2½" × 1¼"
Thwart, oak 1½" × 8"

Seat riser, pine ⅝" × 3"

Well deck, pine 1¼"
Well bulkhead, oak 2"

Frames, oak 1⅜" × 2"

Planking, pine ⅝"

Keel 2¼" × 5½"

1 2 3 4 5 6 7 8 Fod.

Three-masted Spritsail Craft from Aaro

Three-masted Spritsail Craft from Aarø

This type of vessel was built at Assens about 1907. Measurement Project No. 55.
Length: 20 ft 1 in. = 6.30 m
Beam: 6 ft 10 in. = 2.15 m
Height: 2 ft 7 in. = 0.81 m

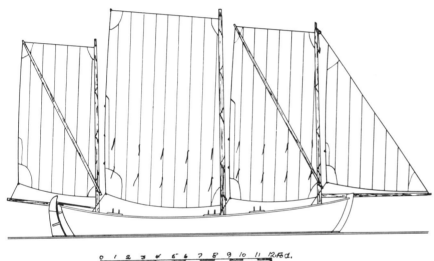

This boat was widely used in fishing with nets and poles in the deep bays off the Little Belt. The herring were driven into the deep trenches of the narrow bays, where they were forced into practical immobility. The net was placed outside the narrow entrance to the trench, and the men would then use their poles to make the shoal swim out and into the net. When several boats were involved at the same time, the fishermen would respect the right of the first comer; he was allowed to set his nets farthest inside, and the others placed theirs farther out.

A crew consisted usually of two to four men. They also caught eel in their seines, and during this type of fishing a jibboom was attached to the bow and one line of the seine was tied to it.

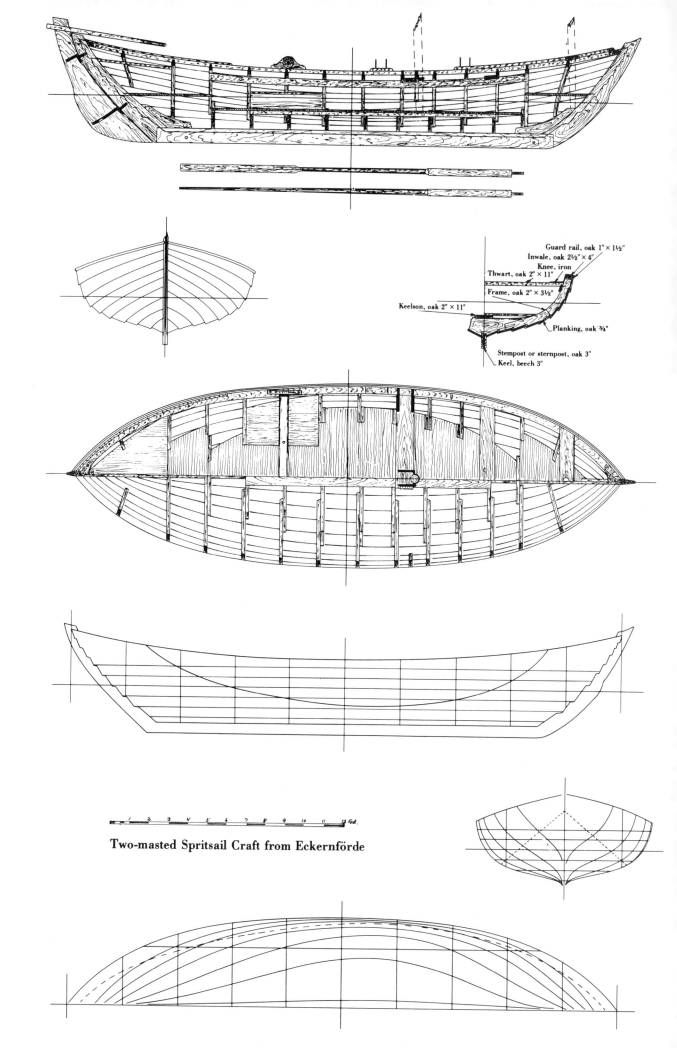

Guard rail, oak 1″ × 1½″
Inwale, oak 2½″ × 4″
Knee, iron
Thwart, oak 2″ × 11″
Frame, oak 2″ × 3½″
Keelson, oak 2″ × 11″
Planking, oak ¾″
Stempost or sternpost, oak 3″
Keel, beech 3″

Two-masted Spritsail Craft from Eckernförde

Two-masted Spritsail Craft from Eckernförde

This type of boat was built at Eckernförde around 1880. Measurement Project No. 49.

Length: 28 ft   0 in. = 8.79 m
Beam: 8 ft 10 in. = 2.77 m
Height: 3 ft   1 in. = 0.97 m
Draft: ca. 2 ft   3 in. = 0.71 m

This boat is a big and solidly built vessel with stepped rabbets, which resulted from each plank having been separately notched into the stem and sternpost in such a way that each extends over the plank below. Thus, the rabbet does not consist of an even curve, but has a stepped outline. The vessel has square looms on the oars, which are inserted between iron tholepins.

Two-masted spritsail craft at Mölteort near Kiel. Drawing by Georg Burmester, 1912.

The boat was exclusively engaged in seine fishing, two boats always working together. When the seine was to be put in place, the men on one boat, which had all the equipment on board, lowered the seine, while the second boat paid out its end of the line. The vessels were then rowed in opposite directions so that the seine would be taut. Then the boats would proceed together in a semicircle, while the seine lines were heaved in on rollers situated aft. The boats would in this way draw the seine together and the catch could be hoisted up and into the vessels. When such boats were engaged in seine fishing, each would usually have a crew of four to six.

Two-masted Spritsail Craft from Halmø

This craft was built at Tåsinge around 1890. Measurement Project No. 12.

Length: 16 ft 0 in. = 5.02 m
Beam: 5 ft 0 in. = 1.57 m
Height: 1 ft 9 in. = 0.54 m
Draft: ca. 1 ft 3 in. = 0.39 m

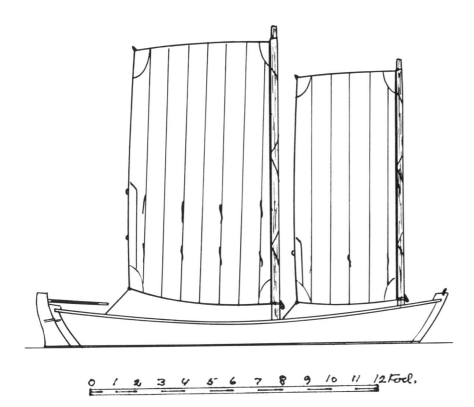

This type of boat, a lightly built craft, was frequently seen in the waters off Svendborg around the turn of the century.

This particular one was built for a farmer on the island of Halmø, and aside from the usual seine fisheries, it was used to ferry schoolchildren and cargo between Halmø and Ærø. Each farm would usually possess a boat of this type, also used by young men and women when they were to attend balls and dances on the surrounding islands.

Facing page: Funeral procession bringing a coffin from Birkholm to Drejø. All the boats are two-masted spritsail craft, and since the wind is dying down they have resorted to use of the oars. Drawing by J. E. C. Rasmussen, 1888, in M. Galschiøt: *Danmark.*

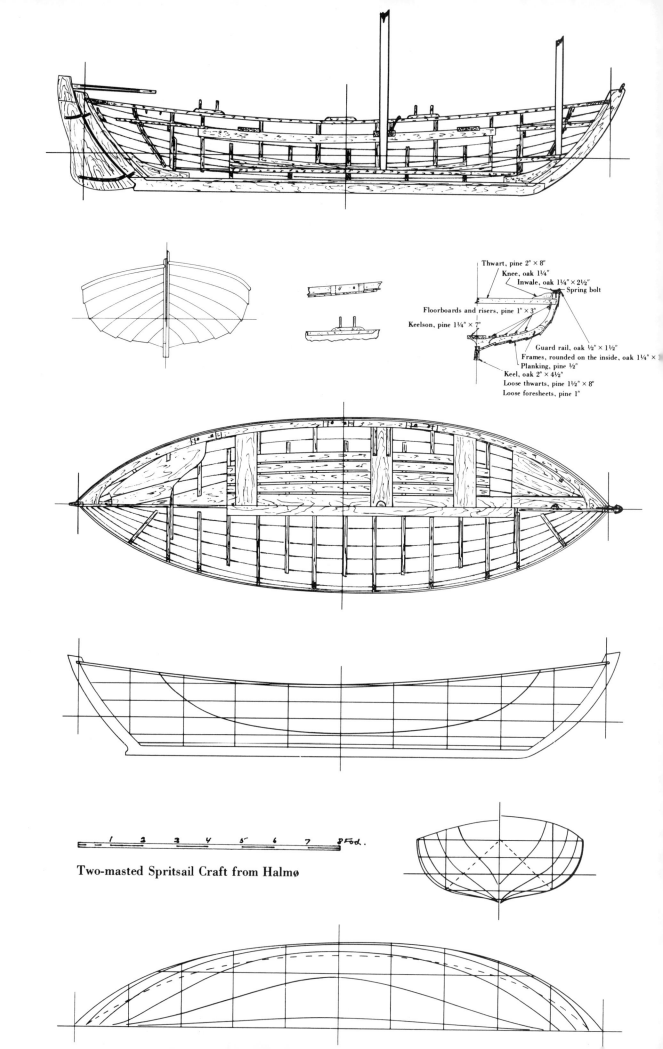

Thwart, pine 2″ × 8″
Knee, oak 1¼″
Inwale, oak 1¼″ × 2½″
Spring bolt
Floorboards and risers, pine 1″ × 3″
Keelson, pine 1¼″ × 7″
Guard rail, oak ½″ × 1½″
Frames, rounded on the inside, oak 1¼″ × 1
Planking, pine ½″
Keel, oak 2″ × 4½″
Loose thwarts, pine 1½″ × 8″
Loose foresheets, pine 1″

1   2   3   4   5   6   7   8 Fod.

Two-masted Spritsail Craft from Halmø

III.
SAILING DRIFTERS

THE VERY NAME OF THE SAILING DRIFTER (*DRIVKVASE*) IN-dicates its two main qualities. First, it is a boat that not only is able to sail but also to drift, and, second, it must be a smack; that is, a boat in which fish can be transported. Normally, to be able to drift was not looked upon as a good characteristic of a boat, but in the case of these special types of vessels it was a necessity whenever the fishing was done with drift seines.

The Fishery

The sailing drifters were used mainly to catch eel. The eel were looked for in places with shallow water and green seaweed, where the long trunk-shaped seine was set in place. The boat, with sails aback, would drift sideways, the seine being fastened with lines attached to the jib-boom and a long spar run out astern. The drifter also had a small spanker aft. In order to drift at a speed of about three knots, the vessel had to have a shallow draft, and the eel smacks were, as a rule, relatively flat vessels built on a plank keel.

In the 1870s a number of Pomeranian families from the area around Barth and Stralsund as well as the island of Rügen emigrated to the southern part of Denmark. These German fishermen brought with them their own equipment and boats and introduced into Denmark the technique of catching eel in drift nets. The reason for this emigration is still unknown, but it is probable that the limits imposed by the German Fisheries Control bodies on the number of fishing boats in many German cities and towns were a contributory cause. Having previously served on boats to which Danish fishermen sold their catches, these foreign fishermen knew well the waters off Småland, which resemble the waters between Rügen and Stralsund. Many Pomeranian fishermen married Danish girls and became naturalized Danes. We see a greater number of examples of such marriages in the years following 1888, when a new Danish fisheries law prohibited non-Danes from fishing along the Danish coasts.

When the fishermen off Småland, who had been using shore and other types of seines, found that the Germans with their drifters caught twice as many eels as they did themselves, they changed over to the German-type vessels and methods. The eel fisheries had always been rather profitable, and any method to make it even more so was welcome. At first, a number of German drifters were purchased through German middlemen, and drifters were also obtained in the various eel-fishing areas. Later on, sailing drifters were built in Denmark, with the German ones serving as models, and in 1894 the boatbuilder Christian Nielsen of Fejø introduced a new type of sailing drifter, which during the following twenty years was sold and used in conjunction with the German drifters.

The Boats

The hulls of the German and Fejø drifters were quite different. Both types had shallow drafts, but the German drifters were very narrow, clinker- or carvel-built boats with flaring bows and elliptical sterns. The old German drifters also had a leeboard on the side in order to be better able to beat to windward; this was later converted to a centerboard, like the one used by the Danish drifters. The Fejø drifters, on the other hand, were clinker-built, sharp-sterned boats with rounded stems, and were often a bit smaller than the German drifters. The rigging was more or less uniform on the two types of drifters.

Drifters were built not only at Fejø but also at Nykøbing on the island of Fyn, at Kalvehave, Marstal, Fåborg, and Kolding. Other kinds of

The round and the concave stems. The sailing drifter on the left with the convex stem is clinker-built, while the drifter with the concave stem is carvel-built. Photograph from Vieregge on the island of Rügen, 1958.

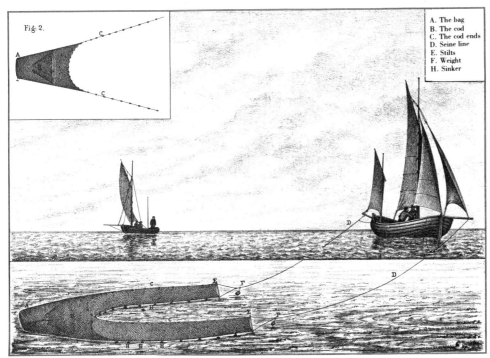

Fig: 2.

A. The bag
B. The cod
C. The cod ends
D. Seine line
E. Stilts
F. Weight
H. Sinker

A sailing drifter with an eel seine. The seine lines are attached to the jibboom and to the spanker boom, while the boat, with backed staysail, is drifting slowly before the wind. At the upper left an eel seine is seen from above. From C. F. Drechsel: *Oversigt over vore Saltvandsfiskerier*, 1890.

boats were adapted for use in the eel-seine fisheries; thus, many herring boats from Nordenhuse had their keels cut off and had a plank attached instead. They were also supplied with a mizzenmast, and thus became ideally suited to drift-net fishing. A number of ice boats from the Great Belt were given a new keel and had a deck added so that they could be used as sailing drifters.

Drifters carrying sails ceased to be built in the years following World War I. Motors were installed and the seines were pulled by the boat instead of the boat drifting with the seine. This method is still in use. However, drift-net fishing was not completely discontinued until after World War II, having experienced a renaissance during the war on account of the unavailability of gasoline for the motors. Aside from seines, traps and weirs were also used along the Danish coasts in order to catch the elusive eel.

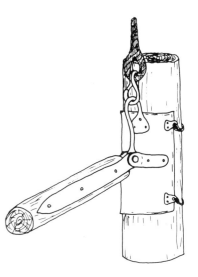

The Crews

The crew on a sailing drifter consisted of a skipper and a boy who was usually called the mate. The skipper was the owner of the drifter and signed the boy on for a longer or shorter period. The boy would be paid in several different ways. He might, for instance, be hired on like the crews on sailing ships, but he might also be allowed to sort out and sell all the smaller kinds of fish that were caught in the seine, in addition to the free meals he had on board. In such cases, the profit from the sale of the smaller fish was the boy's to keep. Alternatively, he might claim a share of the smaller fish in addition to a small wage. Even though the crewmen made very little money in this way, it was not an unusual occurrence for a young man, after having served in the military, to be able to purchase a drifter and start out in life as a skipper.

The Way They Looked

The sailing drifters were painted either gray or green on the outside and had a white bulwark. The colors had no connection with the two nationalities involved, but were used indiscriminately by both German and Danish sailing drifters.

The German Drifter
Minna

The German drifter *Minna* was built at Stralsund in 1872. Measurement
Project No. 9.

Length:	31 ft 6 in. = 9.89 m
Beam:	10 ft 0 in. = 3.14 m
Height:	3 ft 6 in. = 1.10 m
Draft without leeboard:	2 ft 8 in. = 0.84 m
Draft with leeboard:	5 ft 0 in. = 1.57 m

Minna was originally built for one of the German fishermen who later
settled down in Denmark. It was one of the first German drifters to arrive off the southern coasts of the Danish islands.

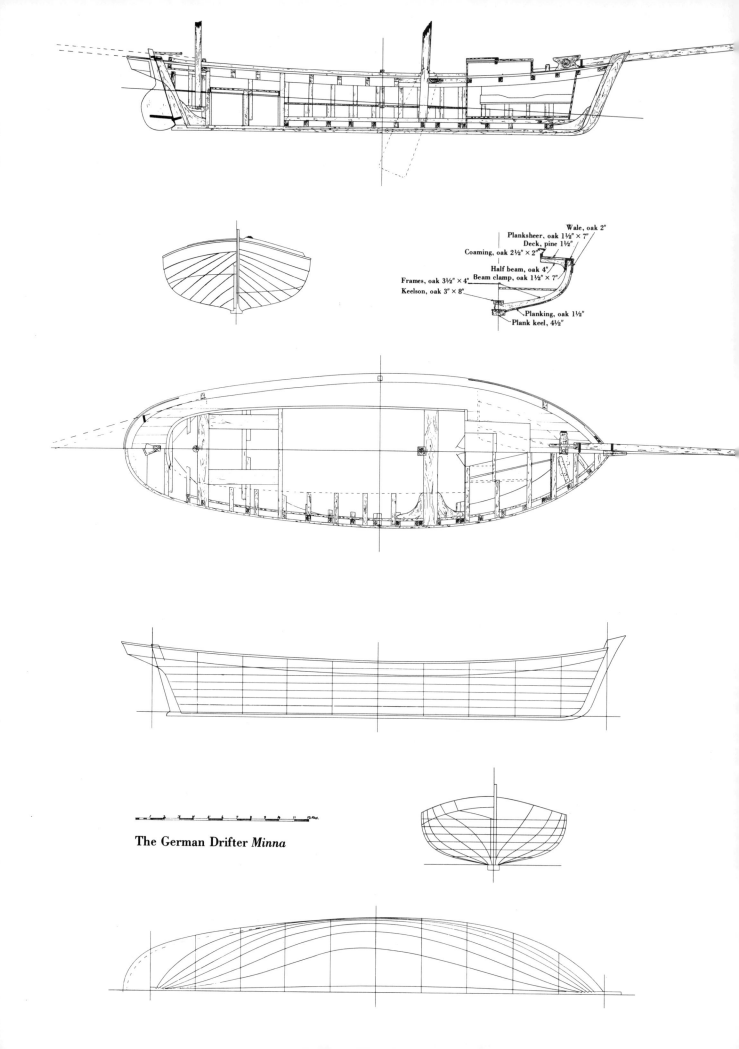

Wale, oak 2"
Planksheer, oak 1½" × 7"
Deck, pine 1½"
Coaming, oak 2½" × 2"
Half beam, oak 4"
Frames, oak 3½" × 4"
Beam clamp, oak 1½" × 7"
Keelson, oak 3" × 8"
Planking, oak 1½"
Plank keel, 4½"

The German Drifter *Minna*

Minna has a well aft and is carvel-built with oak planking; the upper-most plank is called the sheer strake, and it overlaps the next plank below and continues around the stern.

German sailing drifters in the harbor of Ralswiek with eel seines hanging to dry in the masts. Extra staves have been attached to the jibbooms because of the pressure of the seines on the long booms. Photograph from Rügen, ca. 1950.

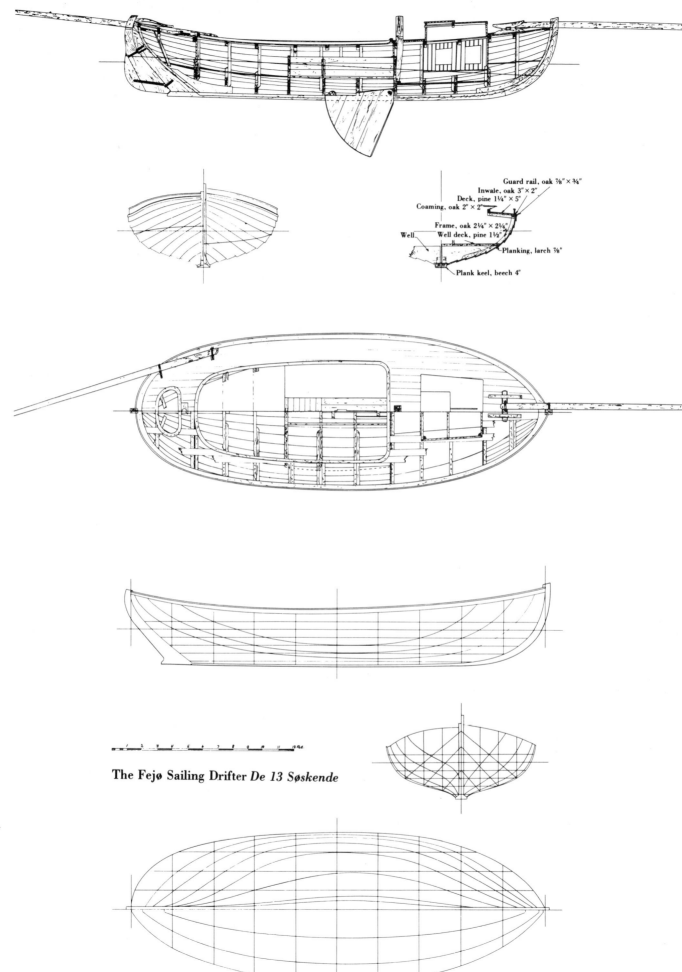

Guard rail, oak ⅞" × ¾"
Inwale, oak 3" × 2"
Deck, pine 1¼" × 5"
Coaming, oak 2" × 2"
Frame, oak 2¼" × 2¼"
Well deck, pine 1½"
Well
Planking, larch ⅞"
Plank keel, beech 4"

The Fejø Sailing Drifter *De 13 Søskende*

The Fejø Sailing Drifter
De 13 Søskende

This boat was built on the island of Fejø in 1911. Measurement Project No. 10.

Length:	27 ft 3 in.	= 8.55 m
Beam:	9 ft 9 in.	= 3.06 m
Height:	3 ft 3 in.	= 1.02 m
Draft with center- board up:	2 ft 6 in.	= 0.84 m
Draft with center- board down:	5 ft 6 in.	= 1.73 m

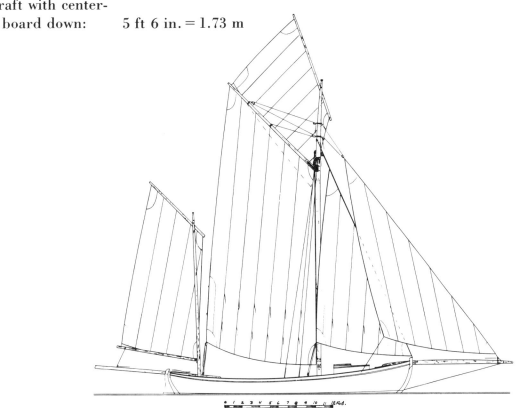

The vessel known as *De 13 Søskende* is a typical clinker-built Fejø sailing drifter with a wooden centerboard.

The shape of the Fejø sailing drifters was created by the boatbuilder Christian Nielsen of Fejø, who has related that he adapted some of the lines of the customs sloops and applied them to the flat drifters. He built not only without drawings and patterns but used only a few shadow molds (which didn't reach all the way out to the planking) as an aid in making the boat symmetrical.

IV.
FJORD BOATS

ALMOST ALL THE DANISH FJORDS, OR BAYS, ARE RATHER shallow draft, and, indeed, most of the fjord boats are either flat-bot-lost their sting before reaching as far as the low-lying beaches. The quiet waters and extensive underwater vegetation make an ideal habitat for eel and herring as well as garfish and flatfish. In order to be able to fish in the shallow waters by the shores, one needs a boat with a very shallow draft, and, indeed, most of the fjord boats are either flat-bot-tomed or smaller shallow-draft boats with keels.

The Limfjord

The government has issued regulations about the fisheries in the Lim-fjord since the Middle Ages. This fjord was the very first area in which fishing was regulated by law, and one of these regulations specified that vessels and their cargoes of fish could pass through the fjord at no charge. The channels must not be obstructed by fishing gear and nets, even in places where the riparian owner has property on both sides of the channel.

Flatner with curved sides and flat bottom. Ribs and spreaders are of rather small dimensions; the strength of the hull is due to the gunwale and the clinker-built hull. Photograph from Glyngøre, 1965.

Before the sea broke through the Agger isthmus in 1825, a huge herring fishery took place there, with Nibe as its center. Following the breakthrough, saltwater fish, such as cod and plaice, appeared in the fjord, while the stock of herring and garfish was considerably reduced. However, the fishermen quickly learned how to adjust to the new circumstances, and following the introduction of the Danish seine at the middle of the nineteenth century the catch grew significantly in relation to the old methods. Moreover, oysters began to make their appearance in the fjord during the years after 1825, and they were soon commercially exploited.

In the narrow eastern part of the fjord, between Løgstør and Aalborg, fishermen would use a vessel called a flatner (kåg), which like the Adrup flatner had a completely flat bottom and was employed in fishing with lines and traps. Seaworthiness was not an important requirement, and the boat managed very well as long as the sea was not too rough. A little farther west, where the fjord became wider, they also used flatners, but these boats had curved, flaring sides and a rather narrow bottom. They were previously used for pole fishing, but since this kind of fishing came to an end, these flatners have been used as pound-net tenders. It took quite some time before this type of fishing became popular, since pound nets were expensive and many fishermen couldn't afford to invest in such equipment. Many of them, therefore, continued to fish with the old seine nets.

The boats known as skiffs (sjægter) are to be found everywhere in the Limfjord; they are smaller keelboats with S-shaped body plans and are decked all around with a ring deck. Easy to handle, these lightweight boats were originally designed for seines worked by hand, but are now used for occasional fishing with hook and line and traps.

Following the introduction of the motor and the growing popularity of the so-called Danish seine, the boatyard at Glyngøre presented a new carvel-built vessel to be used in the Limfjord. It was a narrow type with a straight stem and cruiser stern (Støren of Glyngøre). Boatbuilder Ove Christensen of Glyngøre was a creative personality who worked with a very small staff, including, as a rule, no more than one journeyman and one or two fishermen. He himself would usually concentrate on shipbuilding problems and their solutions. His new boat was one of the first in Denmark to feature a cruiser stern, and its shape and method of construction were completely different from the usual fjord boats, which were clinker-built vessels, lying low in the water, lacking a wheelhouse, and with the motor amidships.

The type, called "pencil cases" (pennalhus) is used for all kinds of fishing in the Limfjord. In the past, the boat was also used in the summertime in the Isefjord and the waters around Skagen. These boats have become very popular, and since there is a regulation to the effect that no fishing boats in the area can exceed five register tons, attempts have constantly been made to make the boats ever bigger without exceeding the prescribed tonnage.

With a somewhat wider beam, Ove Christensen's "pencil cases" have been built to serve as net tenders in most of the places where pound nets are used.

The building of flatners ceased in the middle 1920s, and no new skiffs came from the boatyards after the early 1930s. However, both types of vessel were used as seine boats and tenders for many years after that, but today most are in such disrepair that they are not serviceable anymore. But the "pencil cases" became very popular at the end of the 1920s, and they are still being built in great numbers. Some are no more than sixteen feet in length, and when that small they are usually clinker-built.

The Randers Fjord and Slien

Flatners were also used in many inlets besides the Limfjord. Thus, large flatners were used to ship freight on some of the rivers of Jutland; for instance, the Gudenå and the Randers Fjord. In the North German inlets, long and narrow vessels, very similar to the Gudenå flatner, but many times smaller, were used exclusively for fishing. Such flatners are still in use on the river Slien, but they are now supplied with a motor instead of the old rigging, which was of the same type as that of the spritsail craft.

The Fisheries

The main fishery was the one carried out in the fall, where seine nets were used and the crews of two flatners worked together. When the seine had been placed, the fishermen would tie their flatners to a pole driven into the sea bottom, so that they wouldn't drift in the direction of the seine when it was to be pulled in. Anchors were used instead of poles when fishing with Danish seines.

Slien is divided into several districts, each of which has been assigned a certain maximum number of registered boats. The right to fish belongs to the native families and may only be inherited or sold to fishermen in the area, one result being that their number has greatly diminished. This means an expansion of the rights of those fishermen who are still active.

Flatner from the Limfjord

This flatner was built at Adrup about 1890. Measurement Project No. 80.

Length: 20 ft 0   in. = 6.28 m
Beam: 5 ft 4   in. = 1.67 m
Height: 1 ft 10½ in. = 0.58 m
Draft: 0 ft 7   in. = 0.18 m

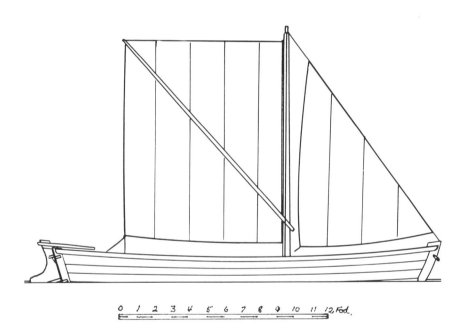

This flatner was constructed on a completely flat planked bottom with transverse cleats fastened through with treenails. Next to the battens are oak side frames. The boat is supplied with a small leeboard, which is placed on the lee side while under sail, so that the flatner won't drift too much to leeward.

The flatner was rowed or sailed by a crew of two, whose favorite method of catching fish was by trapping or angling.

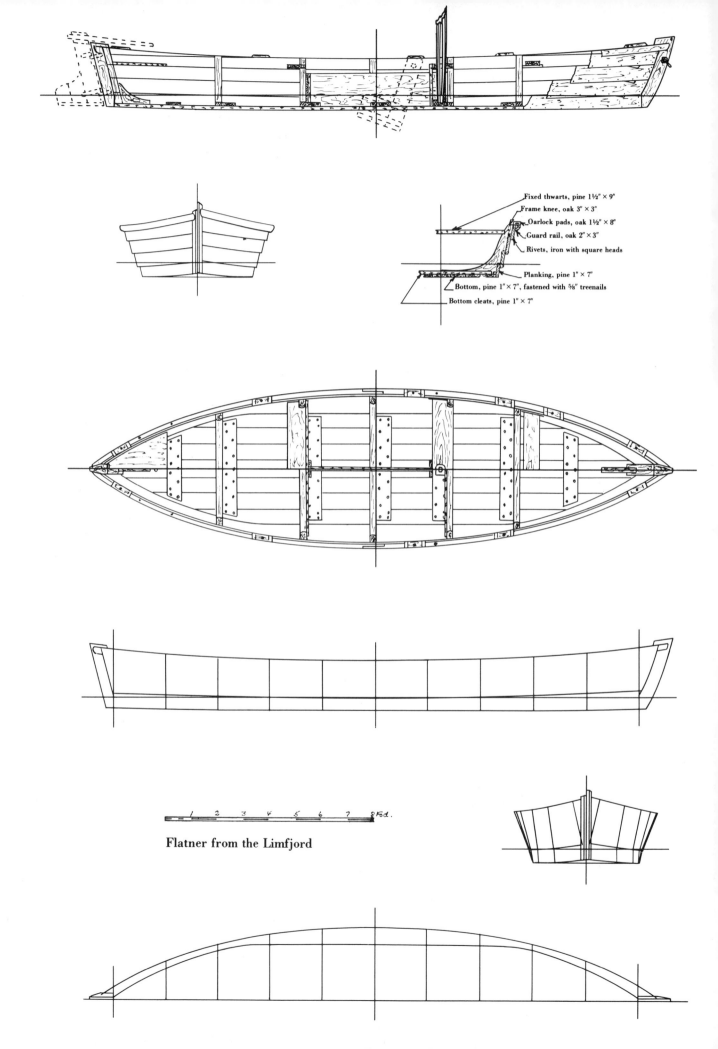

Fixed thwarts, pine 1½″ × 9″
Frame knee, oak 3″ × 3″
Oarlock pads, oak 1½″ × 8″
Guard rail, oak 2″ × 3″
Rivets, iron with square heads
Planking, pine 1″ × 7″
Bottom, pine 1″ × 7″, fastened with ⅝″ treenails
Bottom cleats, pine 1″ × 7″

1 2 3 4 5 6 7 8 Fod.

Flatner from the Limfjord

Flatner from Gjøl Bredning on the eastern part of the Limfjord. The vertical sides and the flat bottom of the vessel are clearly seen in this picture. Photograph from 1965.

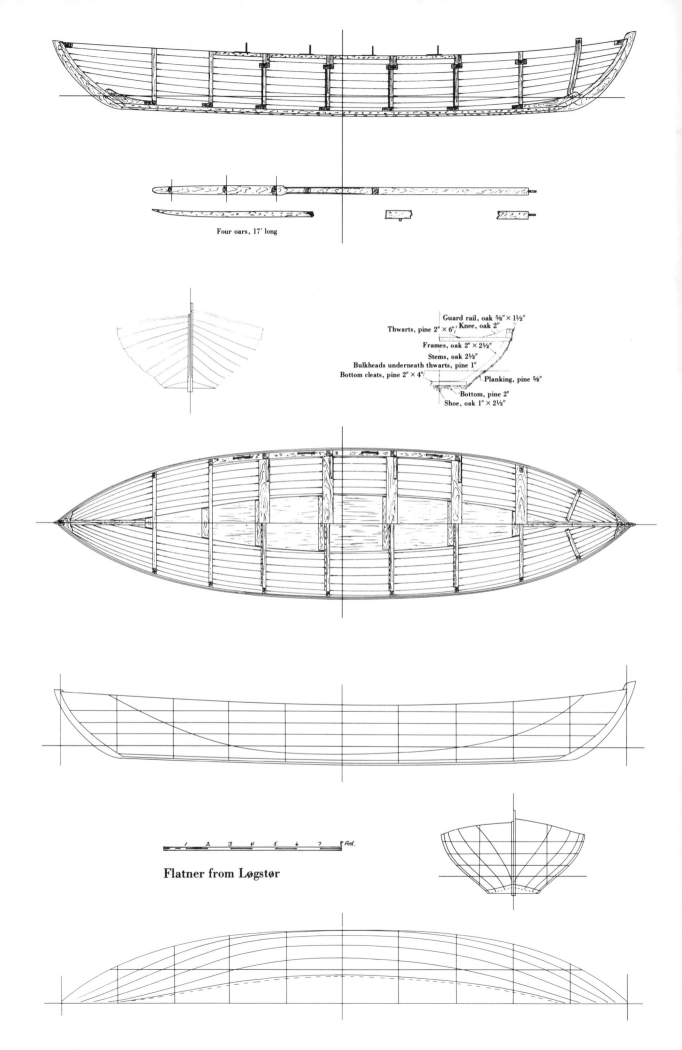

Four oars, 17' long

Guard rail, oak ⅝" × 1½"
Thwarts, pine 2" × 6" Knee, oak 2"
Frames, oak 2" × 2½"
Stems, oak 2½"
Bulkheads underneath thwarts, pine 1"
Bottom cleats, pine 2" × 4"
Planking, pine ⅝"
Bottom, pine 2"
Shoe, oak 1" × 2½"

1 2 3 4 5 6 7 8 Fod.

Flatner from Løgstør

Flatner from Løgstør

This craft was built at Løgstør around 1905. Measurement Project No. 57.

Length: 25 ft   3 in. = 7.93 m
Beam: 6 ft   4 in. = 1.99 m
Height: 2 ft   4 in. = 0.73 m
Draft: ca.   0 ft 10 in. = 0.26 m

The flatner is a narrow, flat-bottomed rowboat, the strong features of which are the flat bottom and the transverse thwarts. Amidships it is furnished with transverse bulkheads, which prevent the cargo from moving about when the wind is increasing. The boat was used in herring fisheries with nets and with poles, and for catching eel.

When rowing a flatner, the fishermen crossed the oars to balance them. The boat was so narrow that if they didn't cross the oars, but rowed in the normal manner, too much of the oar would be outside the boat.

The crew consisted of two, three, or four men.

Flatner on the Sallingsund. The man is rowing with crossed oars. The oars are characterized by their thick and heavy looms. Drawing by Hans Smidt in M. Galschiøt: *Danmark*.

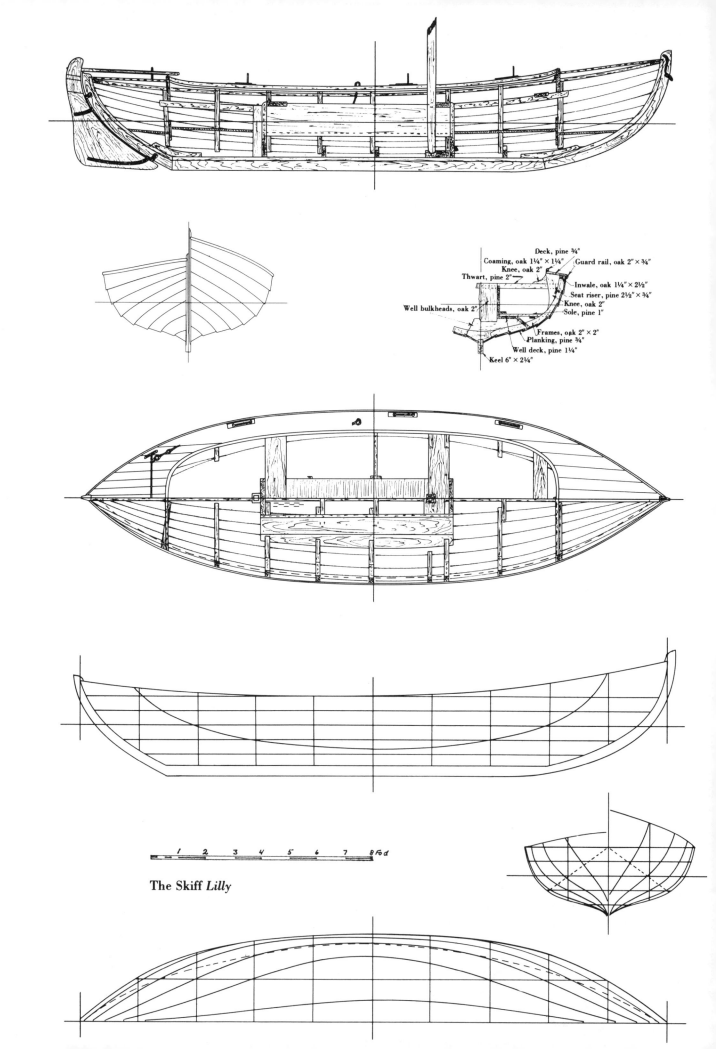

Deck, pine ¾"
Coaming, oak 1¼" × 1¼"   Guard rail, oak 2" × ¾"
Knee, oak 2"
Thwart, pine 2"   Inwale, oak 1¼" × 2½"
Seat riser, pine 2½" × ¾"
Knee, oak 2"
Well bulkheads, oak 2"   Sole, pine 1"
Frames, oak 2" × 2"
Planking, pine ¾"
Well deck, pine 1¼"
Keel 6" × 2¼"

1   2   3   4   5   6   7   8 Fod

The Skiff *Lilly*

The Skiff *Lilly*

The *Lilly* was built on the island of Fur in 1902. Measurement Project No. 59.
Length: 21 ft 0 in. = 6.59 m
Beam: 6 ft 1 in. = 1.91 m
Height: 2 ft 5 in. = 0.76 m
Draft: ca. 1 ft 9 in. = 0.55 m

This type of boat, also known as a skiff, was always a narrow keelboat with a ring deck. It was mainly used for fishing with hand seines, but was also used in fishing with hooks and nets. Over one hundred hand-seine boats have been registered on the island of Fur, but this method of fishing has now been superseded by the use of Danish seines.

Two men and two boys would work together. It was rather common for one of the men to own the boat while the other owned the equipment. They used the oars when setting the seines and used the sails only on the way to and from the fishing grounds.

In the 1880s some fishermen's families moved with their skiffs from the island of Jegindø to Bandholm in the waters off Småland. Here they could make a much better eel catch than previously. They continued the practice of rowing with crossed oars, but this technique didn't become widespread among the fishermen off Småland.

Skiff built by M. Andersen at Agger between 1908 and 1910. The sails are tanned, and the mainsail is sheeted to a deck horse aft. The vessel is now the property of the Limfjord Museum, where this photograph was taken in 1971.

The Glyngøre Boat
Støren

This boat was built at Glyngøre in 1928. Measurement Project No. 62.
Length: 28 ft 8 in. = 9.00 m
Beam: 8 ft 8 in. = 2.72 m
Height: 4 ft 2 in. = 1.31 m
Draft: 3 ft 6 in. = 1.10 m

Støren is a carvel-built boat, with a motor and straight stem and a cruiser stern. It is one of the first of its kind built by Ove Christensen. In Denmark, boats of this type are called "pencil cases." Local fishermen at Glyngøre relate that the name originated at the time the first boat of this type was launched on a Sunday forenoon in 1928. In the afternoon there was to be a race from Glyngøre, with the new boat taking part. A rather large crowd had collected by the harbor, and an older fisherman asked a colleague what kind of ship this strange newcomer was. The latter gave a very indistinct answer, which was misunderstood by the questioner, who exclaimed, "What are you saying? You're calling it a pencil case?"

Since that time, and also perhaps because the boat with its elongated shape may indeed remind one of a pencil case, it has been known under this name, even in advertisements in the newspapers.

Støren was used to catch all kinds of fish in the Limfjord, and was once in a while to be seen off Frederikshavn and Skagen, at which time it lacked a forward deckhouse. The forward deckhouse, the wheelhouse, and the engine compartment were all removable, and the wet well featured narrow slots instead of holes so that it could be used to hold shrimp and eel.

The crew would usually consist of two men.

"Pencil cases" in the harbor at Struer. In the background are seen two net and Danish-seine boats and a North Sea boat on the slipway. Photograph from 1971.

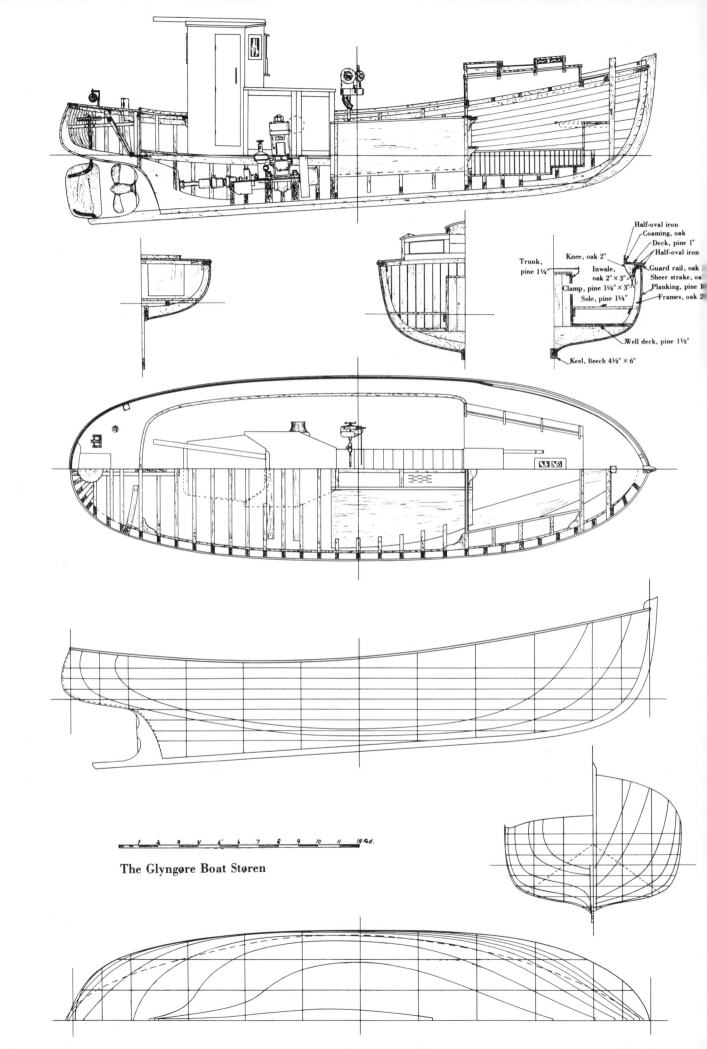

Half-oval iron
Coaming, oak
Deck, pine 1"
Half-oval iron
Knee, oak 2"
Trunk,
pine 1¼"
Inwale,
oak 2" × 3"
Guard rail, oak 2"
Sheer strake, oa
Clamp, pine 1¼" × 3"
Planking, pine 1
Sole, pine 1¼"
Frames, oak 2
Well deck, pine 1½"
Keel, beech 4½" × 6"

1 2 3 4 5 6 7 8 9 10 11 12 Fod.

The Glyngøre Boat Støren

Flatner from Slien

This flatner (*Schlei-Kahn*) was built at Arnæs in 1917. Measurement Project No. 47.

Length: 23 ft 9 in. = 7.45 m
Beam: 4 ft 5 in. = 1.39 m
Height: 1 ft 8 in. = 0.52 m
Draft: ca. 0 ft 6 in. = 0.16 m

The flatner from Slien is a long, flat-bottomed vessel whose bottom consists of two planks, with three narrow planks on each side. It has a leeboard made of iron to prevent drifting. It has been used in the fisheries of Slien from Arnæs to Slesvig.

The fishermen normally steered with a rudder, but when they sailed with the currents they would use a long oar, since the boat would otherwise lie beam-on to the waves.

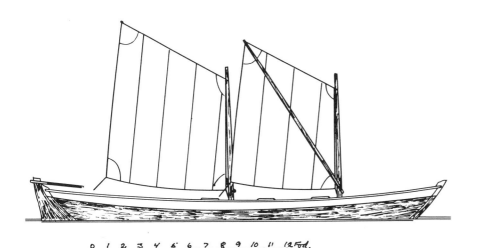

Two German flatners. The fishermen are putting the gear in order following a day of fishing. In the background, a fisherman's half-timbered home. Postcard from 1940.

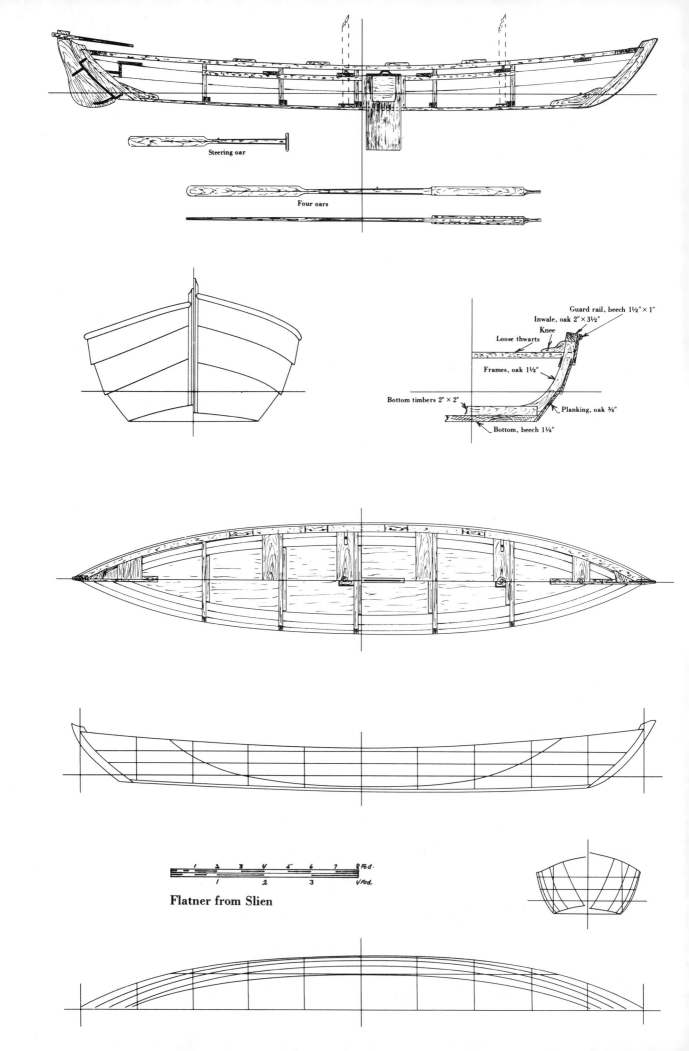

Steering oar

Four oars

Guard rail, beech 1½" × 1"
Inwale, oak 2" × 3½"
Knee
Loose thwarts
Frames, oak 1½"
Bottom timbers 2" × 2"
Planking, oak ¾"
Bottom, beech 1¼"

Flatner from Slien

Flatner from Orø

This flatner was built at Orø in 1920. Measurement Project No. 27.
Length: 14 ft   0 in. = 4.39 m
Beam: 4 ft 11 in. = 1.54 m
Height: 1 ft   6 in. = 0.47 m
Draft: ca. 0 ft   9 in. = 0.24 m

The Isefjord is not very different from the Limfjord, but it is somewhat smaller. One can sail across its broadest part in a few hours, which means that the boats used do not have to be very big in order to be found seaworthy; the kind of fishery engaged in and the depth of the water are the factors to be taken into consideration when selecting a boat.

Fishing with lines and traps was carried out in the inner part of the Isefjord, and when conditions were favorable the fishermen would also spear eels, which was looked upon not only as work but also as a sport. The only big island in the bay, Orø, has for centuries been mainly devoted to agriculture, and it has been a natural thing for the farmers who had fishing rights to have small boats lying on the beach, with which they might supplement the income derived from the farm. Such a flat-bottomed flatner from Orø has been an ideal boat in which to negotiate the shallow and narrow channels surrounding the island.

The Orø flatner is of a very plain and simple design. Such vessels may be built by anyone without special expertise in the craft of boatbuilding. The one pictured here, for instance, was built by a house carpenter on the island. The bottom and the sides are planked with pine.

It was used for occasional fishing, and not fitted with sails; it was rowed or poled by one man.

Fishing by torchlight on the Odense Fjord. Eel are being speared from a number of dinghies, as also was done in the waters around Aerø and in the Isefjord. The fishermen stand in the stem and row slowly forward with the eel spear. When they see an eel in the light of the carbide lamp, they try to spear it with a lightninglike downward motion. Such spearing could only take place at night and with a calm sea. Drawing by Rasmus Christiansen, 1887, in M. Galschiøt: *Danmark*.

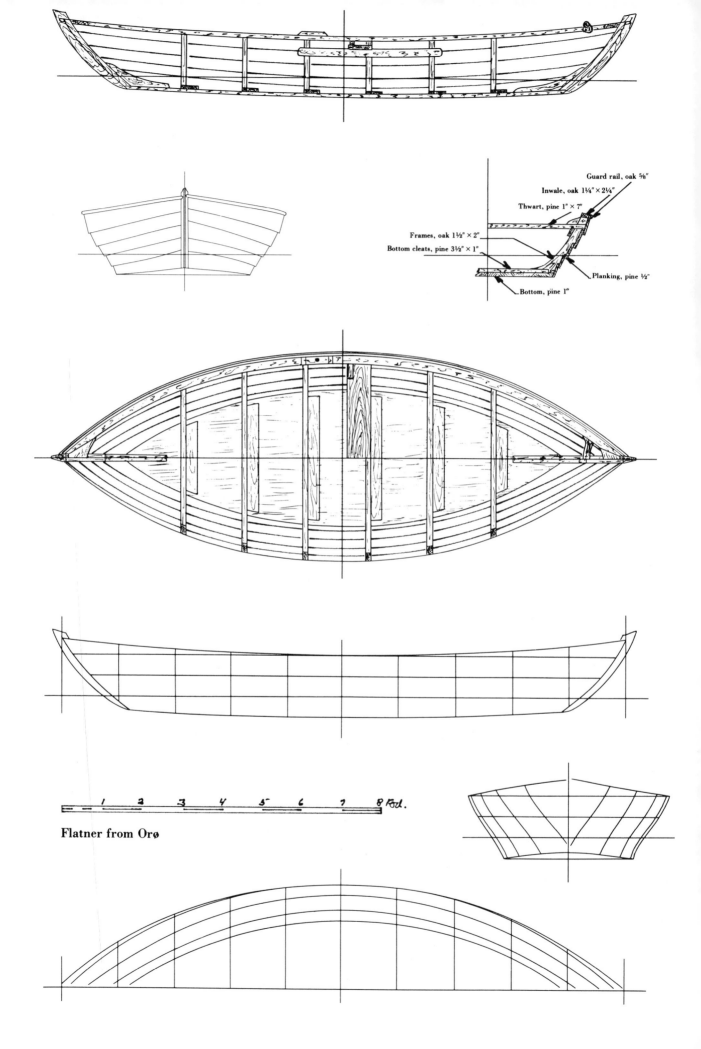

Guard rail, oak ⅝"

Inwale, oak 1¼" × 2¼"

Thwart, pine 1" × 7"

Frames, oak 1½" × 2"

Bottom cleats, pine 3½" × 1"

Planking, pine ½"

Bottom, pine 1"

1   2   3   4   5   6   7   8 Fod.

Flatner from Orø

Dinghy from Lynæs

This dinghy was built at Lynæs in 1918. Measurement Project No. 30.

Length: 11 ft 8   in. = 3.66 m
Beam: 4 ft 9   in. = 1.49 m
Height: 1 ft 8½ in. = 0.54 m
Draft: ca. 1 ft 0   in. = 0.31 m

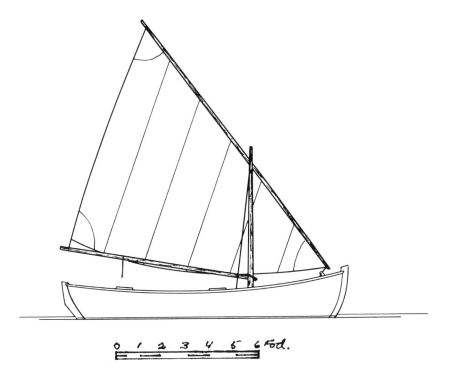

The towns of Frederikssund and Lynæs have for the last hundred years been well known for the small boats built by their master shipwrights. The Frederikssund dinghy was the creation of Ole Jensen, a pilot who, at the middle of the nineteenth century, stayed an entire winter at Lister in southern Norway and there learned the fine points of boatbuilding. When Ole Jensen returned to Denmark, he started to build small dinghies that early on gained fame for their low cost and seaworthiness. Many fishermen from the northern part of Sjælland lost their lives during the hurricane of 1852. This catastrophe was the main reason that impelled Ole Jensen to make an effort to improve the existing fishing boats, most of which had been built in Sweden, at Mölle and Rå on the coast of Scania. These vessels were flat and narrow, and, in pilot Jensen's view, were not good sailers and far from seaworthy enough for the

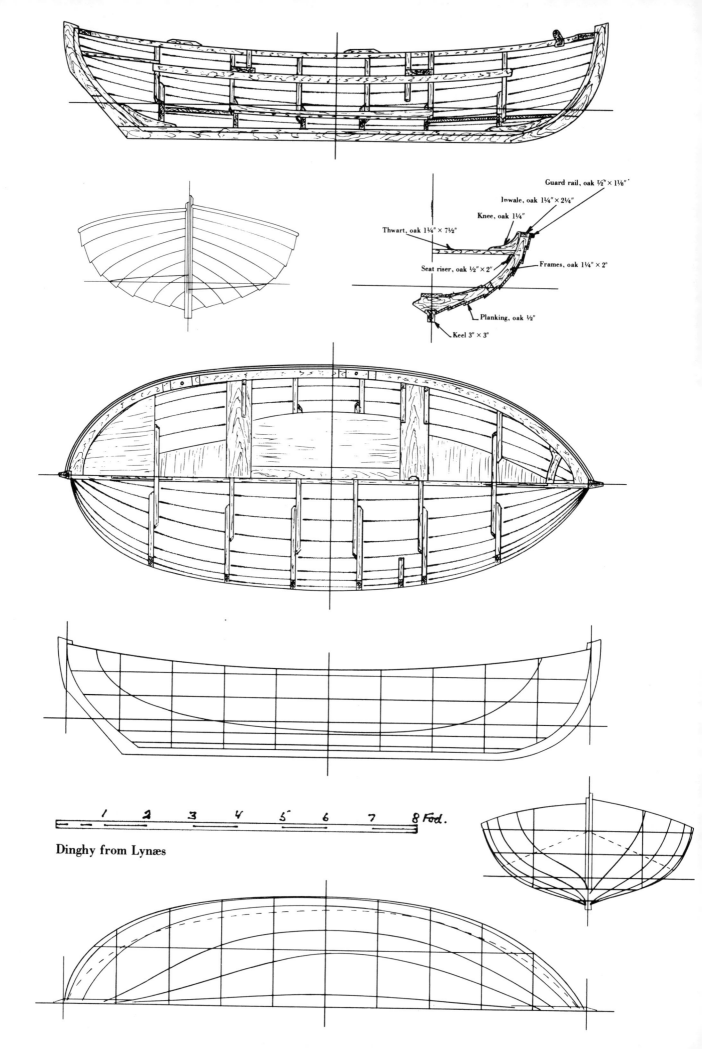

Guard rail, oak ½″ × 1⅛″

Inwale, oak 1¼″ × 2¼″

Knee, oak 1¼″

Thwart, oak 1¼″ × 7½″

Seat riser, oak ½″ × 2″

Frames, oak 1¼″ × 2″

Planking, oak ½″

Keel 3″ × 3″

1   2   3   4   5   6   7   8 Fod.

Dinghy from Lynæs

rough seas in the Kattegat. Ole Jensen built, with his small dinghies as patterns, a few bluff-bowed, decked boats with fine lines below the water, which greatly surpassed the Swedish boats in seaworthiness and became very popular. The Frederikssund dinghies completely supplanted the Swedish boats and were also used in the lighthouse and pilot services.

This type of dinghy has been built by many different shipwrights along the bay. The shape was further adapted by a builder named Madsen at Lynæs; he became widely known for his Lynæs boats and dinghies, which were fuller above the water than the older boats. The small Lynæs dinghies, which are still being built, are used for occasional fishing and duck-hunting as well as for spearing eels. Prior to the time that the biggest fishing vessels were equipped with rubber life rafts, these dinghies were also used as lifeboats. The old Isefjord dinghies were always built without any patterns, and during the last few years their shape has been transferred to plastic forms at a small yard at Lynæs, which now produces standardized fiberglass dinghies in a few different sizes.

The Lynæs dinghy is a bluff-bowed vessel built of oak. It is usually painted white, with tarred bottom, and it may be rowed or sailed using a lateen sail.

Lynæs dinghy with a lateen sail. The dinghy is heavily laden with children. The steering is done with a long oar astern. The top of the very short mast is seen behind the sail. Photograph from 1925.

V. NORTH SEA BOATS

> The vessels that are used to fish cod and haddock are mainly open boats as far as the Danish west coast is concerned, since due to the lack of harbors and places of safety they must be built in such a way that they can be pulled up on shore, and as far as the other waters are concerned, the fisheries are conducted so close to shore, or in such enclosed waters, that decked vessels are not needed. It is only from Esbjerg, Fanø, Hjerting, and to a slight degree Frederikshavn and Grenaa that cod fishing is carried out with decked vessels.

Thus wrote fisheries consultant C. F. Drechsel in 1888 about the cod and haddock fisheries. He also informs us that the fishermen on the west coast used open boats that they had to pull up on the beach, since there were no harbors.

The reflections made by Drechsel are manifestations of a viewpoint grounded in cultural geography. The relations between natural conditions and man's activities and tools illustrate a problem that exists wherever man utilizes natural resources. The cultural geography of Denmark's west coast, facing as it does the North Sea, is, as far as the boats are concerned, quite complicated but very interesting, and that is the reason that the boats in this section will be presented in what might be called geographical order, as distinct from the preceding sections, in which the vessels were classified according to use.

Natural Conditions

The Danish North Sea coast consists mostly of flat beaches with sand dunes and a hinterland that usually has very sparse vegetation. Outside the beaches there are two or three sandbars parallel with the coast. On these sandbars the water is very shallow at ebb tide, but otherwise the depth of the water increases gradually the farther out one goes. Since the west wind is so predominant in Denmark and since the coast is

Facing page: A shore seine is being pulled in by fishermen aided by a few women. The boat used to set the seine is lying at the beach. *Inset:* A fisherman with the belt to which is attached the horizontal seine line. From C. F. Drechsel: *Oversigt over vore Saltvandsfiskerier,* 1890.

a. Rope for hauling
   seine ashore
b. Bridles
c. Supports
d. Sleeves
e. Gills
f. The bag

completely unprotected as it faces the North Sea, the waves and the swell are often very powerful. The waves are tamed by the flat beaches, which are covered by ice in the middle of winter, and along which there are often rather strong currents. Fishing from small boats has been the rule along the entire North Sea coast, and the boats had to be so small that they could be hauled up on the beach by one or two men.

We might suppose that these rather uniform natural conditions along Denmark's west coast would result in somewhat the same kinds of boats being built. The logical thing would have been for the fishermen, after having fished in the same area for hundreds of years, to have arrived at the best type of boats in regard to seaworthiness, suitability, ease of handling, and price. This, however, is not the case, for the types of boats built prior to the turn of the century had only two things in common: they were modestly equipped and they were low-priced. Flatners and boats with both flat bottoms and pronounced keels were used and hauled up on land when the work was done.

The Boats

Characteristic of this period were the flatner from Hjerting, the flatner from Vorupør, the boat from Klitmøller, and the boat from Hvide Sande, which were all used for long-line fishing or fishing with shore seines. The boat from Hvide Sande is considered to be the oldest type among these boats.

At the end of the last century boats were also used such as the boat from Løkken, which was a bigger boat with splendid sailing qualities. It is said that such boats have even been used to sail as far as the southern part of Norway. Just before the turn of the century, one could read in the periodicals published for the fishermen about attempts being made in several places along the coast to improve the existing types of vessels. Thus, many open boats from Harboøre were decked in 1899, and in the year 1900 a boat from Harboøre drifted ashore at Vorupør, where the local fishermen became so enthusiastic about it that they sent for a boat-builder and asked him to take down the measurements of the boat so that he could make them one like it. At Løkken, in 1890, a boat of almost two tons was built for Lønstrup, about which it was said that many unfortunate accidents might have been avoided if the fishermen down there possessed as fine boats as those of the fishermen at Løkken. Thus, we see that attempts were indeed made along the North Sea coast to improve the boats, and many fishermen who could not afford to buy a new boat put a canvas deck on their old boats, or a deck of plain wooden planks, in order to prevent the spray from entering the boat.

The situation must have been more or less like this on the west coast when the fishermen of Harboøre in 1901, copying some motor vessels that had been shipwrecked, introduced new and bigger boats with flat bottoms, a dagger board, and a motor. Later accounts indicate that these attempts were successful, and this new type represented by *Marie* of Søndervig together with another motorized boat opened a new chapter in the North Sea coast fisheries.

The fishermen at Harboøre had motors added to their boats at the same time that the first motor was put in a Danish seine boat at Frederikshavn, where the fishermen at that time were supposed to have a special ability to appraise innovations in their field. Thus, we can't very well regard the fishermen along the North Sea coast as being a conservative lot, opposed to new developments. The slow progress made in introducing better types of boats on the west coast must rather be seen in relationship to the minimal resources, the few marketing outlets, and the consequent lack of ready cash among the fishing population.

The Fisheries

The fisheries along Denmark's west coast in the old days consisted mainly of fishing for cod and haddock, carried out with hooks and lines, or with a jig and a line. The shore seine is also an ancient piece of equipment, with which the fishermen mainly caught groundfish.

A long line was about three hundred fathoms long, and rope ends with attached hooks were fastened to it at certain intervals. Before the line was set in the water, it was coiled on a wooden tray, and the four to six hundred hooks, after being cleaned, were arranged in a corner of the tray. As bait, they used either sand worm, liver, or pieces of herring. In such a ground-line fishery, which in the old days was conducted in the fall and from February to Pentecost, all the lines belonging to the crew members were tied together and made into one long line, which was placed athwart the current and anchored with a grapnel or a large stone. The fishermen worked as teams consisting of two to nine men. This kind of fishery did not require boats bigger than a flatner or a dinghy; the boats never had wells, since the fish were dead when they were brought aboard. Each fisherman had two sets of lines, so that one set could be prepared with hooks at home while he himself was at sea.

Jigging was a kind of fishing that took place all year round, mainly by old men and boys. The equipment was very simple, consisting merely of a line with a shiny jig, or spoon hook, which was rhythmically raised and lowered in the water until it was swallowed by an eager fish.

The shore seine was an old and very effective net, which consisted of

a. Hook
b. Leader
c. Line
d. Grapnel (rock)
f. Buoy

Fig: 1.

Fishing with hook and line. Two men in a boat are tending a line yielding a good catch. The line has been anchored at both ends, but one anchor and most of the line have already been taken in. After C. F. Drechsel: *Oversigt over vore Saltvandsfiskerier*, 1890.

a trunk-shaped seine with two long lines. It was widely used by the boats on the west coast that went far out to sea and were big enough to have both seines and lines on board. This kind of shore-seine fishery was very much in use among the fishermen and farmers on the flat coasts of the district of Vendsyssel.

When setting the seine, the rope end of one line would be fastened ashore, and the boat with the seine would be rowed at an angle perpendicular to the coast, while the line was paid out. When there was no more line to pay out, the fishermen placed the seine in the proper position and rowed back to shore with the other line. The boat was moored on the beach and the men divided into two teams, each of which began to pull in their lines. This work might take several hours, and the next trip out could not be attempted until the entire seine was ashore and the fish were on the beach. The operation was preferably begun in the middle of the night, if the wind was blowing in the right direction, and it was important to get to the beach first and lay claim to the best spot. If they could set the seine three times, it was considered a good day's work.

In the middle of the 1870s some fishermen from Skagen began to use small shore seines, called hand seines. After rowing out from shore and placing the seine, they would drop anchor and pull in the seine with two men at each side of the seine. This method was similar to the one used when fishing with a Danish seine; the fishermen considered it to be very advantageous not to be dependent on the shore.

The Organization of the Work

The west coast fishermen were not very affluent, and it was a rare occurrence for a man to own a boat as well as its equipment. The men would join together in order to benefit from the group's work and investment. In the case of flatners and small boats, one or two fishermen might own the vessel, having at the same time joined one or two others who only owned long lines. The lines were always personal property, which the owner had to keep in repair himself. When fishing with seine nets from larger boats, each man received a share of the catch. The fishermen on one vessel would be members of a company or a team, and each grown man owning equipment would get one full share, as did the boat itself. Men who didn't own any equipment might receive a half share. Boys and women who helped with pulling in and coiling received a quarter share. Each man in the group was obligated to bring a certain number of seine lines, marked with a certain sign or letter, which he was to keep in good repair himself. People outside the fishermen's circle might purchase parts of the seine and receive a certain fraction of the catch, while fishermen without any equipment could also get involved and receive proportionately smaller proceeds. There were also a number of farmers and merchants who invested money in boats as well as seines and rented it all to fishermen in return for certain shares in the catch.

Selling the Fish

The fishermen of the Danish west coast usually had few good opportunities to sell their catches. With their small boats, they were not able to bring the fish to exporters in the fishing harbors and quickly dispose of their haul.

The fish would usually be brought ashore in the fisherman's home area; it was divided on the beach among the different partners, who had to take care of the selling themselves. Some of the fish was eaten at home, but in order to earn some money for other staples it was necessary to sell as much of it as possible. To the west coast fishermen, the most important thoroughfare on land was the beach, on which they could drive their wagons, although with some difficulty, and there were not many roads inland. A good share of the fish was therefore exported to foreign countries by being bought up by German and Dutch smacks, which had already contacted the fishermen out on the open sea or rode at anchor along the coast. This kind of sale had the advantages that the purchasers paid with ready cash and the fishermen were not obliged to clean the fish themselves. Of the catches that remained in the country, some were sold to the farmers, many of whom would bring their wagons down to the beach, but the fishermen's wives would often have to clean the fish themselves and then offer them for sale up at the farms.

Salt has always been a good preservative for foods, and much herring was salted along the west coast; some of this herring was used in the fishermen's own homes, while a good part was sold. A great improvement was gained in the opening in 1874 of the railroad service along the coast via Varde and Esbjerg to Lunderskov, and in 1878 from Lemvig to Vemb. The lightly salted fish could thus be transported by rail to consumers in a much larger area. Later, large quantities of fish were sold

A Hvide Sande boat used as a roof over a toolshed. The use of boats as roofs of sheds occurred in several areas, but in this case the boat has been covered with cement to make it even more watertight. The boat is now owned by the Danish National Museum. Photograph from 1965.

every week to Germany at fixed prices. The fishermen also used to smoke the fish in their chimneys or, on dry days, outdoors. Some would render oil from the cod livers and sell it to the apothecary, and when someone in the southern part of North Jutland caught lobsters in his seine, they were kept in well boxes until they could be brought to the market at Thisted.

The Fishermen

What kind of people were these offshore fishermen? We don't know very much about them, other than that they were a people who had settled in modest wooden or half-timbered houses among the dunes and in the hinterland. Many of them had small farms, for in the old days in Denmark there were few fishermen who could make a living from the sea alone. From the church records we know that they would often starve and that in very cold winters receive some public support. During the summer months, when there was little fish in the ocean, many of them worked on the inland farms from the time of Midsummer Day till Michaelmas. But the fishermen did not enjoy this sideline, since as workers paid by the day in the haying and harvesting seasons they earned less in a week than they could make in a day when the fishing was good.

The farmers did some fishing themselves. In the church records of Rær, Pastor L. Mehr wrote that in 1893 five men drowned during an attempt at landing their boat. Of these five, two were farmers, two were smallholders, and one was a cottager. Which ones were also fishermen and which were merely farmers is very hard to determine. From the protocols of the officials who recorded shipwrecks, we find that fishermen would often take home with them wreckage and would keep valuables from a shipwreck, but when necessary risked their lives to rescue the crews whose ships had been wrecked by storms.

We may conclude that the people living along Denmark's North Sea coast, in their harsh geographical environment, worked hard to make a living, and that they were exposed to many dangers; we also know that they must have been incredibly skillful in sailing their boats. To be able to sail a boat across three sandbars and up on the beach, without being pulled back by the undertow, is an art that one ought to learn while still a child. In order not to get stuck on the sandbars, one may often, having passed the first one, have to lie still and wait for a big wave that will carry the boat across the next bar. If the boat happens to lie athwart the waves, one may be sure of capsizing or at best having the boat fill with water. The art of sailing one's boat up on a sandy beach is an ancient one, which has at times been conducted as a sport, but on the North Sea coast there are people who still engage in it out of necessity.

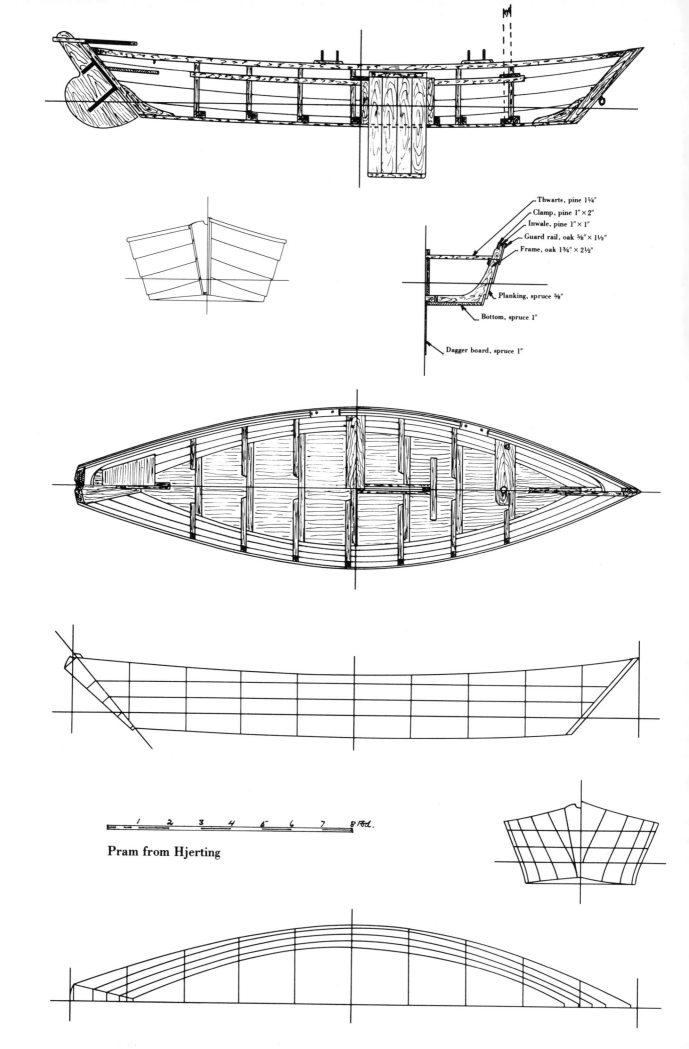

Thwarts, pine 1¼"
Clamp, pine 1" × 2"
Inwale, pine 1" × 1"
Guard rail, oak ⅝" × 1½"
Frame, oak 1¾" × 2½"
Planking, spruce ⅝"
Bottom, spruce 1"
Dagger board, spruce 1"

1   2   3   4   5   6   7   8 Fod.

Pram from Hjerting

Pram from Hjerting

This boat was built at Hjerting around 1930. Measurement Project No. 63.

Length:	18 ft	4	in. = 5.75 m
Beam:	5 ft	0	in. = 1.57 m
Height:	1 ft	11½	in. = 0.61 m
Draft without leeboard:	0 ft	9	in. = 0.24 m
Draft with leeboard:	2 ft	6	in. = 0.79 m

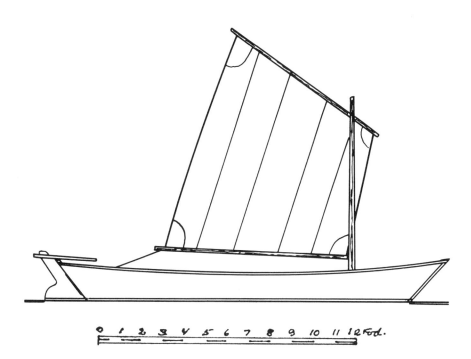

The pram from Hjerting was built of spruce and was of simple design, with a slightly rockered bottom held together by transverse cleats of oak. It often had a small lugsail and featured a dagger board in order to reduce drifting while under sail. The pram, which is of a type very popular in the area around Hjerting, was used to catch fish with hook and line, nets, and traps, in addition to the spearing of eels.

The shape of the Hjerting pram was supposed to have been introduced into Denmark by Kristian Thomsen, a ship carpenter, who during his travels had seen the dories of the Newfoundland fishermen. These dories were used to fish with lines in the Atlantic, with schooners as mother ships. When he later settled in Hjerting, he built many of these dories, which were called Hjerting prams. (In Denmark, the term *pram* just means a simply built boat.) A. L. Jensen, a coach builder, took over the boatyard, and with his sons he built a considerable number of them, which even on the North Sea coast have proved themselves to be seaworthy craft.

The bottoms and garboard plank were tarred black, the two next planks were green, and the sheer strake and gunwale were black. Thwarts, the foresheets, and the dagger board case were tarred and were painted green.

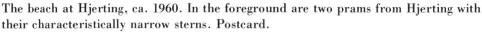

The beach at Hjerting, ca. 1960. In the foreground are two prams from Hjerting with their characteristically narrow sterns. Postcard.

Pram from Vorupør

This type of pram was built at South Vorupør about 1895. Measurement Project No. 67.
Length: 15 ft 0 in. = 4.71 m
Beam: 5 ft 3 in. = 1.65 m
Height: 2 ft 0 in. = 0.63 m
Draft: ca. 1 ft 0 in. = 0.31 m

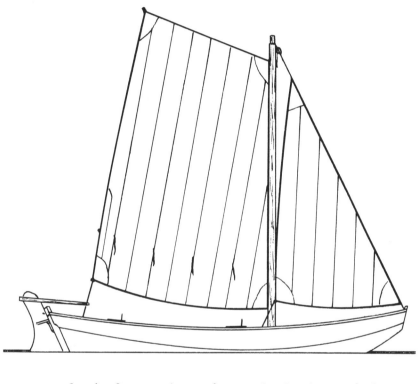

This type, which is called a Norwegian pram not only by local fishermen but also throughout Denmark, was built in three different sizes, with lengths of fifteen, eighteen, or twenty feet. It was used along the North Sea coast from Hirtshals to Agger. It is a full-bowed and solid-looking pram with good cargo-carrying capacity, and is used for fishing with hook and line and occasional fishing along the coast.

The lapstrake planking, which in this pram is of spruce, runs smoothly from the stern to the stem, except for the fourth plank, whose forward end must run out to a taper.

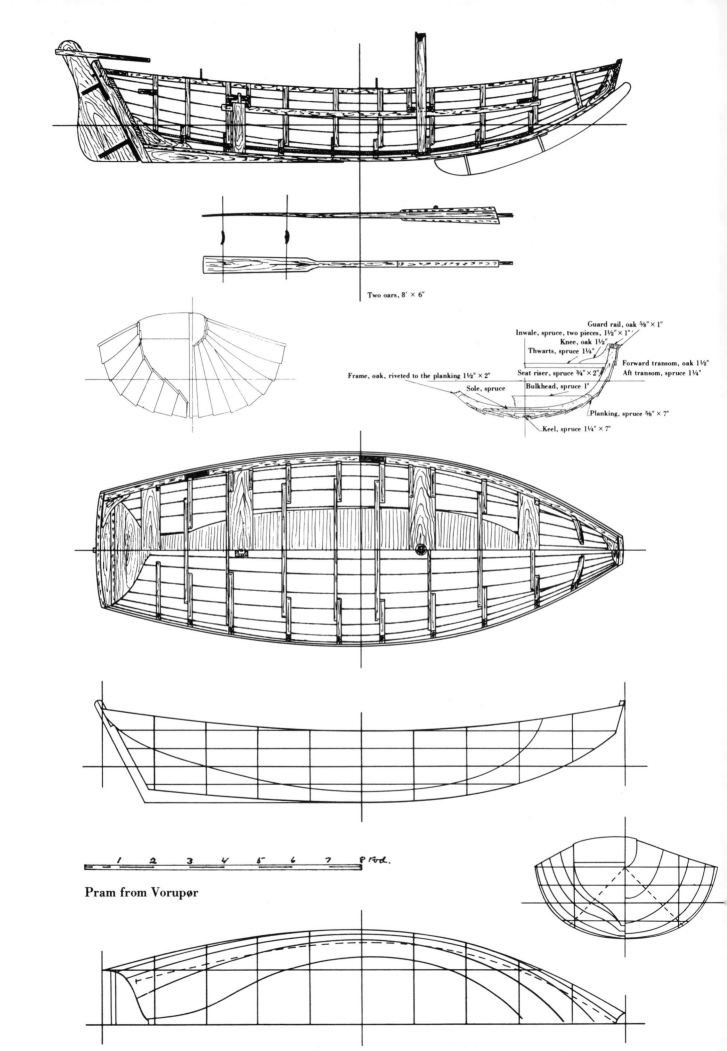

Two oars, 8' × 6"

Guard rail, oak ⅝" × 1"
Inwale, spruce, two pieces, 1½" × 1"
Knee, oak 1½"
Thwarts, spruce 1¼"
Forward transom, oak 1½"
Aft transom, spruce 1¼"
Frame, oak, riveted to the planking 1½" × 2"
Seat riser, spruce ¾" × 2"
Sole, spruce
Bulkhead, spruce 1"
Planking, spruce ⅝" × 7"
Keel, spruce 1¼" × 7"

1   2   3   4   5   6   7   8 Fod.

Pram from Vorupør

The pram is equipped with a removable fin which, with the aid of a tiller that can be slipped onto the top, can be adjusted in such a way that it will aid the boat in keeping closer to the wind. As in most other North Sea coast boats, the afterthwart contains a pump with a pump case, which has outlets on both sides of the boat and may be used no matter to which side the boat is heeled. The pram is designed with a triangular stern, to whose upper edge is fastened an additional plank that gives one a good grip when the boat is launched. Some fishermen also maintain that the plank prevents the waves from breaking over the stern when the boat is pushed up on the beach.

Prams and coastal boats on the beach of Vorupør. In the foreground, a number of prams; on the right, an old hand winch. In the background, the motor house with an electric winch for the larger boats. Postcard from 1960.

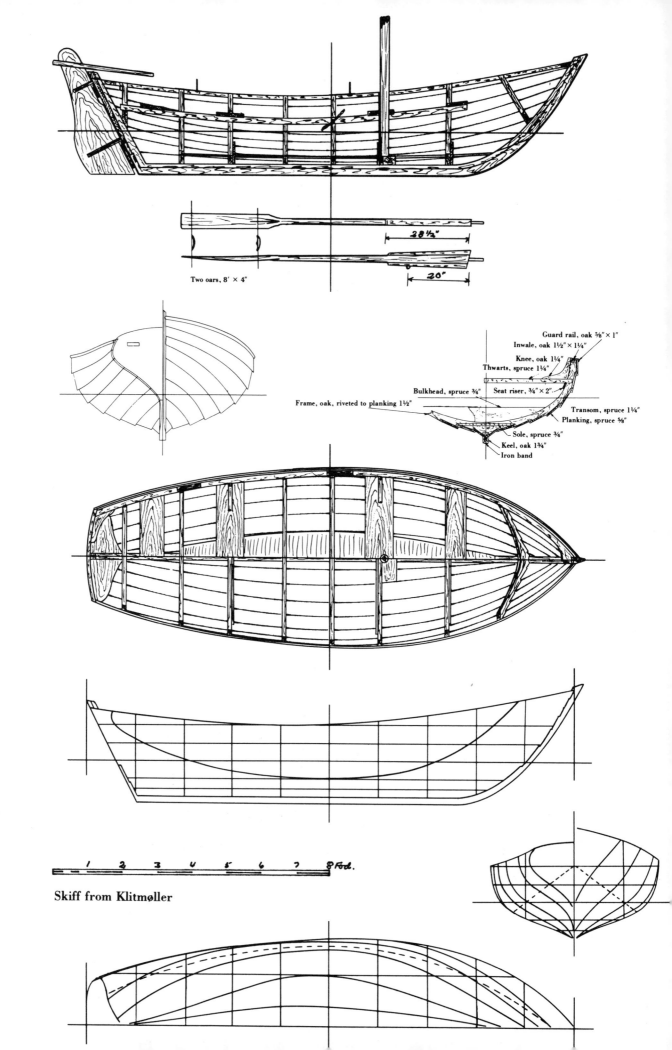

Two oars, 8′ × 4″

Guard rail, oak ⅜″ × 1″
Inwale, oak 1½″ × 1¼″
Knee, oak 1¼″
Thwarts, spruce 1¼″
Bulkhead, spruce ¾″   Seat riser, ¾″ × 2″
Frame, oak, riveted to planking 1½″
Transom, spruce 1¼″
Planking, spruce ⅜″
Sole, spruce ¾″
Keel, oak 1¾″
Iron band

1   2   3   4   5   6   7   8 Fod.

Skiff from Klitmøller

Skiff from Klitmøller

This type of skiff was built at Klitmøller around 1905. Measurement Project No. 68.

Length: 14 ft   0 in. = 4.39 m
Beam: 4 ft 10 in. = 1.52 m
Height: 2 ft   0 in. = 0.63 m
Draft: ca. 1 ft   3 in. = 0.39 m

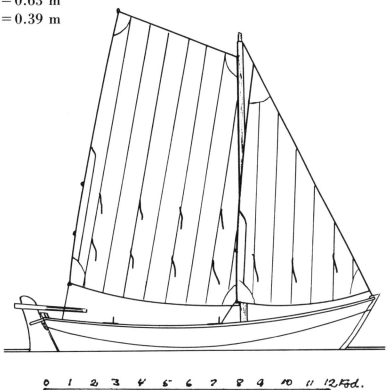

0 1 2 3 4 5 6 7 8 9 10 11 12 Fod.

The Klitmøller skiff is a stiff little boat with a rakish stem. This type has been used primarily along the coast from Vigsø to Klitmøller, the latter being the North Sea coast port where the water depth most quickly increases from the foreshore out. It is a good sailer and is faster than the round-bottomed prams. The rabbet is stepped at the stem, while the ends of the planks in the stern are cut off flush with the transom.

The skiff was the same color as the pram. The two uppermost planks were tarred, and these planks, in addition to the gunwale, the floorboards, and thwarts, were painted green; the other inboard woodwork was tarred and gleaming black.

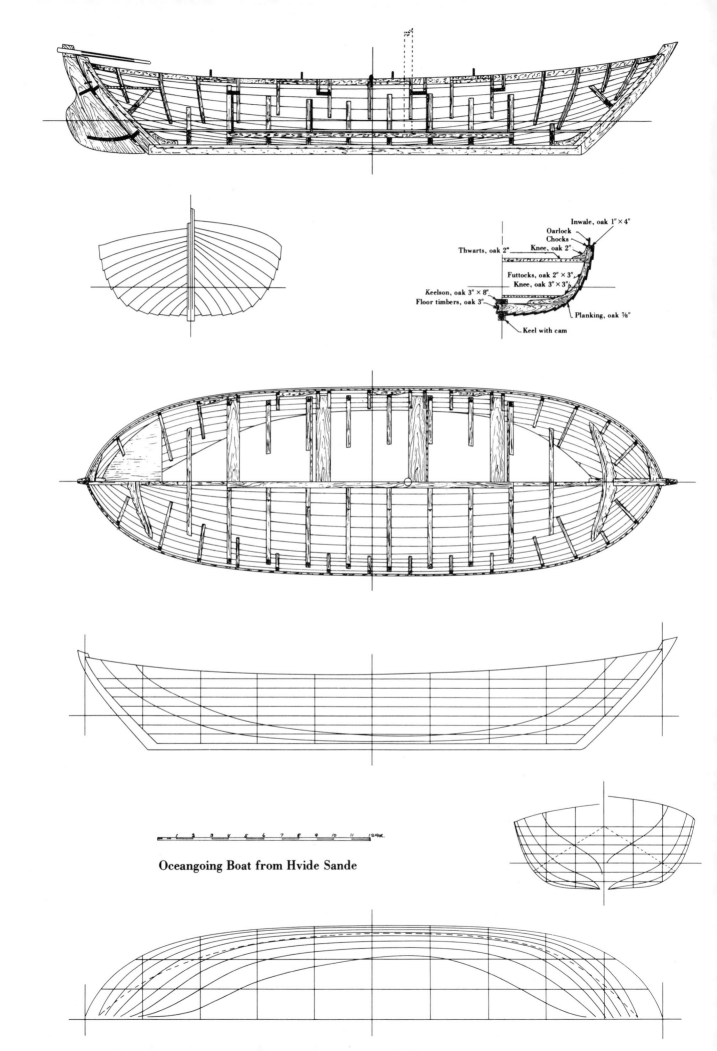

Inwale, oak 1″ × 4″
Oarlock
Chocks
Thwarts, oak 2″
Knee, oak 2″
Futtocks, oak 2″ × 3″
Knee, oak 3″ × 3″
Keelson, oak 3″ × 8″
Floor timbers, oak 3″
Planking, oak ⅞″
Keel with cam

Oceangoing Boat from Hvide Sande

Oceangoing Boat
from Hvide Sande

This boat was built at Stadil around 1870. Measurement Project No. 64.
Length: 32 ft 5 in. = 10.17 m
Beam: 10 ft 2 in. = 3.19 m
Height: 3 ft 9 in. = 1.18 m

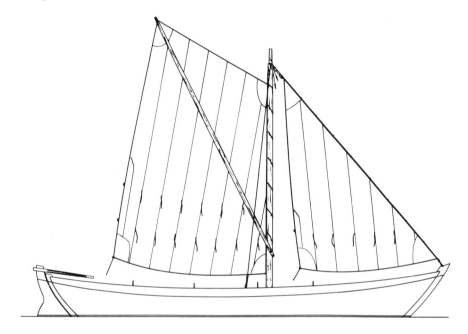

This boat is straight-keeled and built of oak, and the planks are fastened together with iron rivets, but fastened with treenails to the ribs.

In 1938, the boat was placed on top of a toolshed (see page 96) to act as a roof and was covered with cement, in which the owner has made an inscription that tells about the boat's use. It says, *inter alia*, that the boat was used for fishing as well as for carrying cargo. Andreas Jensen of Hvide Sande, an auctioneer, purchased the vessel in 1912 and took down the mast and rigging, so that it might be used as a barge to be towed by a motorboat, and it carried cargo in the Bay of Ringkøbing until 1931, at which time this commerce was taken over by trucks. The boat was transferred to the National Museum in 1966.

This oceangoing boat was tarred on the outside and inside, with the exception of the sheer strake. which was painted white.

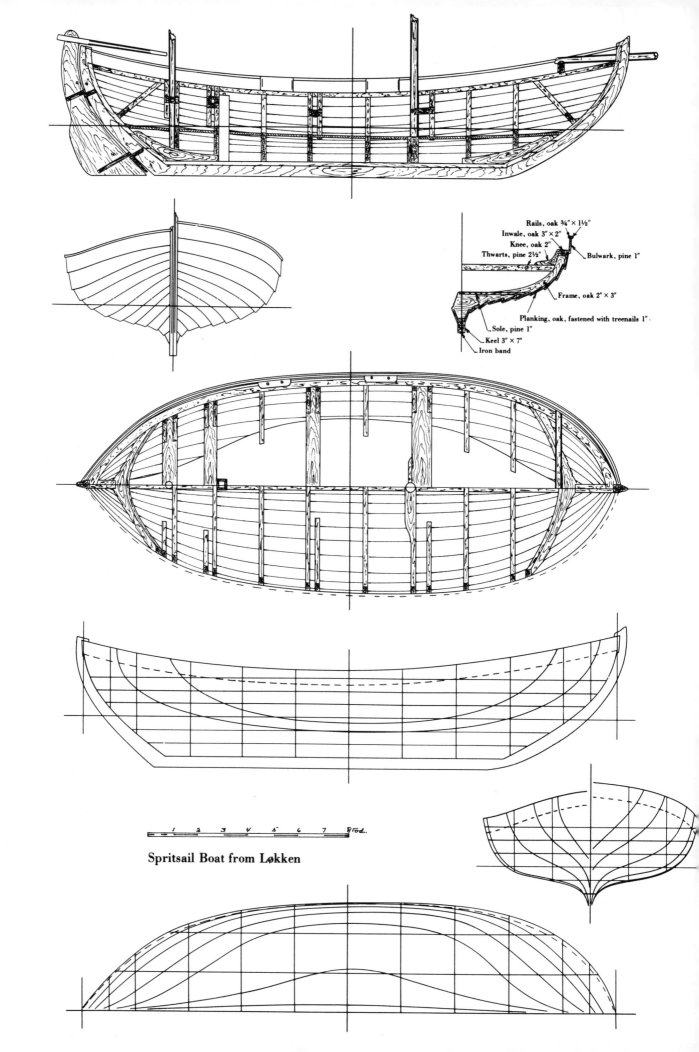

Rails, oak ¾" × 1½"
Inwale, oak 3" × 2"
Knee, oak 2"
Thwarts, pine 2½"
Bulwark, pine 1"
Frame, oak 2" × 3"
Planking, oak, fastened with treenails 1"
Sole, pine 1"
Keel 3" × 7"
Iron band

1 2 3 4 5 6 7 8 Fod.

Spritsail Boat from Løkken

Spritsail Boat
from Løkken

This type of spritsail boat was built about 1886. Measurement Project
No. 71.
Length: 21 ft 1 in. = 6.62 m
Beam: 8 ft 5 in. = 2.64 m
Height: 3 ft 4 in. = 1.05 m
Draft: ca. 2 ft 0 in. = 0.63 m

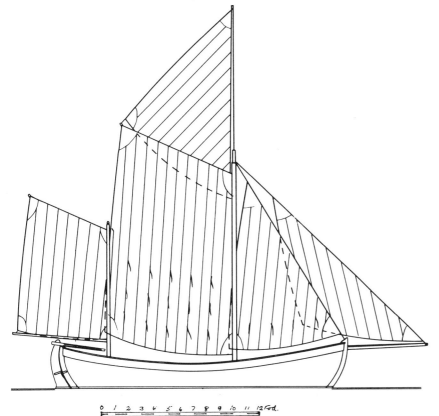

The boat from Løkken is of shallow draft and is built of oak, the planks
being fastened to the ribs with treenails. It is a robust, seaworthy vessel,
with an efficient rig, and it has been used for fishing as well as cargo
carrying. It reminds one, to some extent, of the boats that—probably
inspired by the Limfjord sloops—appeared at the same time at Harboør
and Holmslands Klit.

It was rebuilt in 1903 and given a deck and deckhouse, and was also
fitted with a motor.

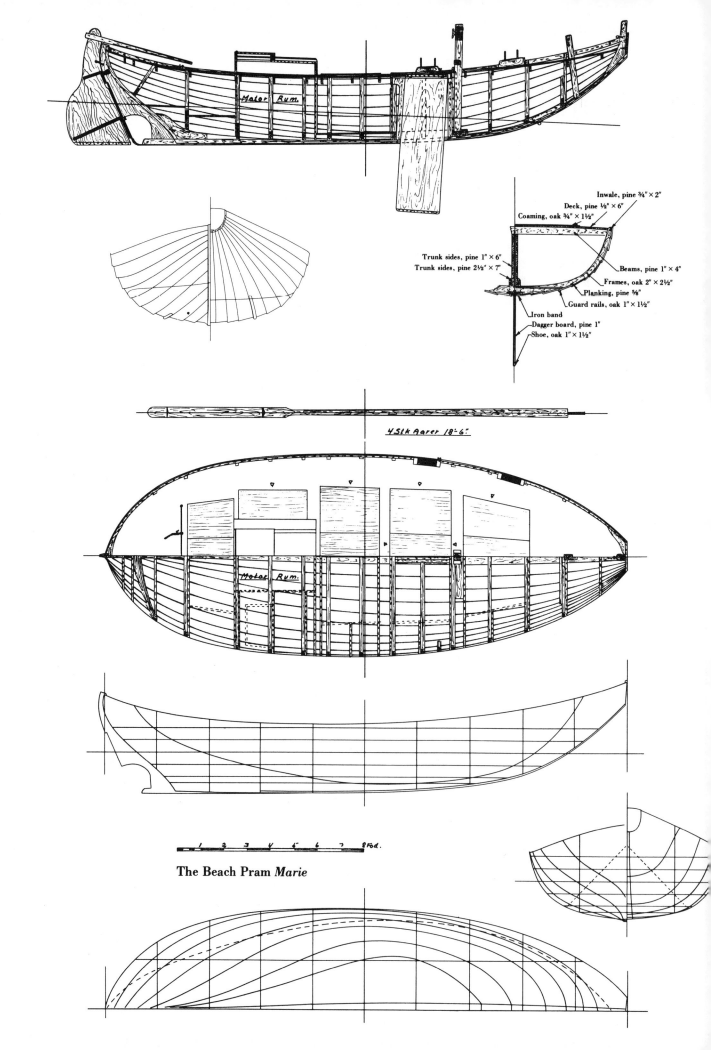

Inwale, pine ¾" × 2"

Deck, pine ½" × 6"

Coaming, oak ¾" × 1½"

Trunk sides, pine 1" × 6"

Trunk sides, pine 2½" × 7"

Beams, pine 1" × 4"

Frames, oak 2" × 2½"

Planking, pine ⅝"

Guard rails, oak 1" × 1½"

Iron band

Dagger board, pine 1"

Shoe, oak 1" × 1½"

4 Stk Aarer 18'-6"

Motor Rum.

1 2 3 4 5 6 7 8 Fod.

The Beach Pram *Marie*

The Beach Pram *Marie*

The *Marie* of Søndervig was built at Nørre Lyngvig in 1929. Measurement Project No. 66.

Length: 22 ft 2 in. = 6.96 m
Beam: 8 ft 3 in. = 2.59 m
Height: 2 ft 9 in. = 0.86 m
Draft without
   leeboard: 1 ft 9 in. = 0.55 m
Draft with
   leeboard: 4 ft 0 in. = 1.26 m

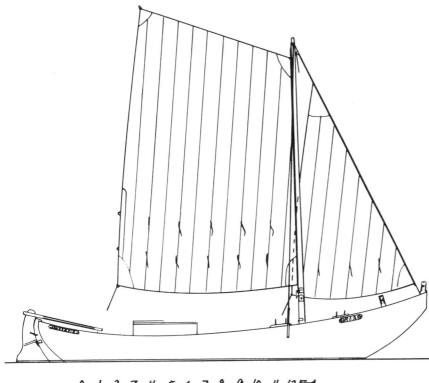

0 1 2 3 4 5 6 7 8 9 10 11 12 Fod.

This pram is built like a Norwegian pram forward, but with a sharp stern, and it has both sails and a motor.

This type of pram was used with or without a motor and some were open boats, while others had a half deck. The pram was used for fishing along the coast from Limfjord to Nymindegab. The fishermen consid-

An open boat of the same type as *Marie* of Søndervig. Photographed in the harbor of Hvide Sande in 1965.

ered it to be a seaworthy vessel, more popular than other boats of the same size.

Cod, flatfish, and mackerel were fished from this pram. The hatch behind the deckhouse was used when the fishermen were angling, and the hatch forward of the mast was used for equipment and whenever the boat was rowed. There were usually four men on board when they fished with nets, since two men were needed to stand in the midship hatches to pull the nets over the gunwale; one man had to stow and one had to do the steering.

The *Marie*, like the spritsail boat from Løkken, was painted white on the outside and had a black bottom. The deck was light gray, and the coamings, hatches, and the interior woodwork were tarred gleaming black.

THE EXPANSION OF THE FISHERIES

THE LATER PHASES THAT THE SHORE FISHERY OF THE North Sea coast has gone through have occurred together with the development that took place in the various ports. It must be seen in light of the more protected location of Hjerting and Esbjerg and the rapid technological development of the fisheries based at Frederikshavn.

The fishing village of Fladstrand in 1805 got its own small-boat harbor, which during succeeding years grew at a rapid pace on account of its being used as a base for gunboats during the war with England. The town was granted a municipal charter in 1818, and Frederikshavn (as the town was rechristened) became the base for the fisheries in the Kattegat and the Skagerrak. Frederikshavn has, since that time and up to World War I, been the town in North and West Jutland with the largest fishing fleet.

The first decked vessel intended for deep-sea fishing was built in the 1870s in the yard of a shipwright by the name of Buhl. It was reported about then that the Danish seine had been used at Hals for the first

Danish-seine cutter *N. I. Laursen* of Frederikshavn. One of the old, big cutters that were made unprofitable by the "sharks." The cutter is moored in the harbor with flags and all sails set. From a catalog from the motor manufacturing firm of Alpha, ca. 1906.

time; the newly built decked vessel was, indeed, to be equipped with this new type of fishing gear. In the late 1880s the shipyards at Frederikshaven concentrated solely on round-sterned fishing vessels of twenty to forty tons, and these seagoing boats became very popular under the name "the Frederikshavn type." The town at that time expanded greatly in size, due to the growing fishing industry and the artisans and craftsmen involved with it, such as blacksmiths, sailmakers, ropemakers, and seinemakers. The fishing off Iceland was also begun around the turn of the century. Some fishermen from the North Sea coast and others from Skagen (the Skaw) settled in town in order to make a better living, and several Swedish herring boats used to unload enormous quantities of fish in the harbor.

In 1891 and succeeding years, several fishing vessels had motors installed; prior to that, some of them had been equipped with steam winches to haul in the seines. The year 1900 marked the start of the practice of installing small internal-combustion engines in the boats attached to the fishing vessels, making it unnecessary to row when seines were to be put in place. A rather large boat was always used to put the seine in place. Having arrived at a promising spot, the fishermen would have the vessel ride at anchor, put the seine and the lines into the boat, which would take the line out as far as it would go, place the seine, and then return to the vessel, where the men would haul in the lines with the winch. When the seine had been emptied, it would be reset at a different angle, and thus they would, in time, cover all points of the compass. When there were no more fish to be had in a large circle around the boat, they would weigh anchor and stop in another promising spot and repeat the process.

The cutter *Gorm* was built in 1904–1905. It was considerably smaller than the ordinary Danish-seine cutters, but in contrast with these others it was designed to place the seine all by itself. This was a new technique, and *Gorm* and its many successors of this type came to be called "sharks." The "sharks," of which a few had been clinker-built prior to *Gorm*'s appearance, were much easier to maneuver than the fishing boats and outstripped the latter by dint of their more powerful engines and greater effectiveness. The smaller boats thus became superfluous in this type of fishing and were sold to villagers along the coast as far as Lønstrup. Here they were used in the more modest hand-seine fishing and, in time, superseded the Løkken type of boats. Their most important feature, as far as the fishermen were concerned, was their motor, and together with boats like *Marie*, which was rather an enlargement of the pram from Vorupør, they came to represent the beginnings of a more systematic fishery along the coast. The seagoing boats with motors and the smaller Danish-seine fishery were dominant, but the catching of lobster in special lobster pots was also on the increase.

The Cutter *Gorm*

This cutter was built at Frederikshavn in 1904–1905. Measurement
Project No. 3.
Length: 32 ft 9 in. = 10.28 m
Beam: 12 ft 0 in. = 3.77 m
Height: 6 ft 0 in. = 1.88 m
Draft: 5 ft 6 in. = 1.73 m

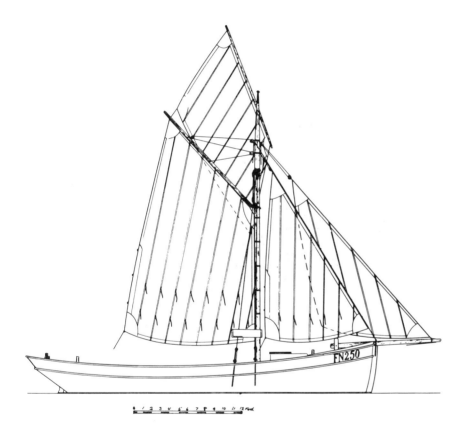

Gorm is said to have been the first "shark" that was carvel-built, and it
was considerably smaller than the old Danish-seine cutters, which, following the appearance of the "sharks," lost out in the competition. The
advantage that the "sharks" had over the others was the fact that they
were independent of the small boats, since they placed the seine all by
themselves after having fastened the end of one of the lines to a buoy.

Even this early, we see that the installation of a motor leads to
smaller sails. On *Gorm*, the mainsail boom was completely dispensed
with in order to provide more working space on the deck around the
well.

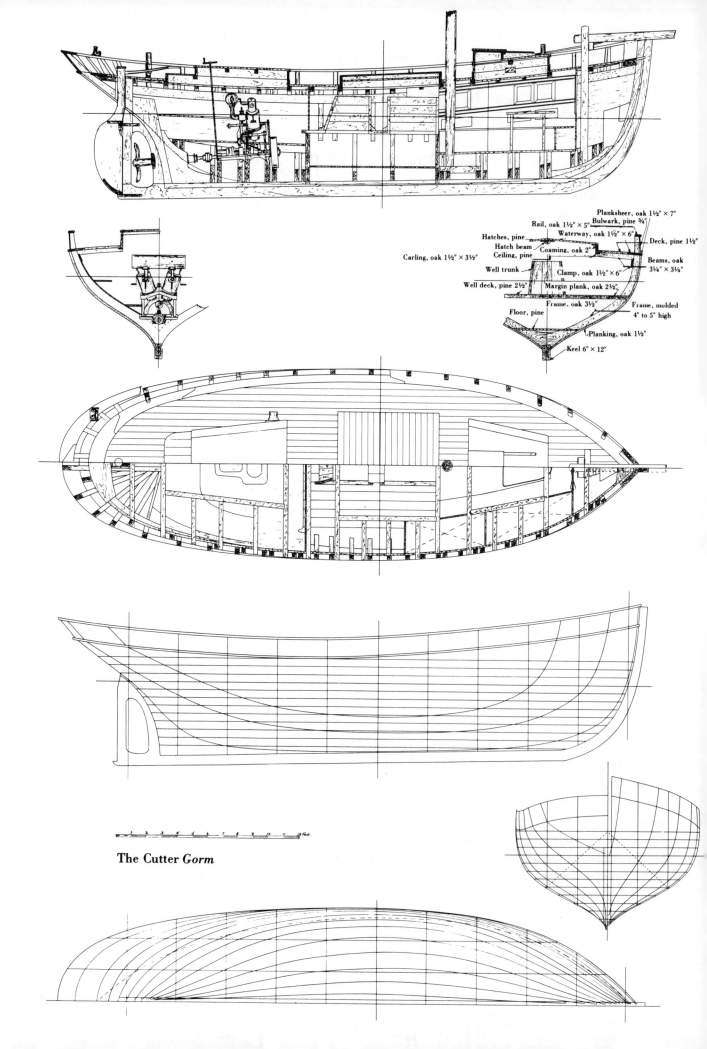

Planksheer, oak 1½″ × 7″
Bulwark, pine ¾″
Rail, oak 1½″ × 5″
Waterway, oak 1½″ × 6″
Hatches, pine
Deck, pine 1½″
Hatch beam
Coaming, oak 2″
Carling, oak 1½″ × 3½″
Ceiling, pine
Beams, oak 3¼″ × 3¼″
Well trunk
Clamp, oak 1½″ × 6″
Well deck, pine 2½″
Margin plank, oak 2½″
Frame, oak 3½″
Frame, molded 4″ to 5″ high
Floor, pine
Planking, oak 1½″
Keel 6″ × 12″

The Cutter *Gorm*

The *Gorm* had a crew consisting of the three owners and a boy. The fish caught included dabs, haddock, and plaice. The seine lines were pulled in with the roller at the stern, aided by the winch at the side of the motor's deckhouse.

The topsides, the bulwark, and the deckhouse were painted white, and the roof of the house and hatches were painted gray. The plank-sheer, the waterway, and the deck were varnished.

Gorm was equipped with a two-cylinder Alpha motor, similar to the one shown above. The two cylinders were set on a slant and made a V. From the catalog of the motor manufacturing firm of Alpha, ca. 1906.

The cutter *Føniks* of the "shark" type. The wheel has been placed about midships and forward of it a bulwark to protect the helmsman has been constructed. From a catalog with Russian text from the motor manufacturing firm of Alpha, ca. 1906.

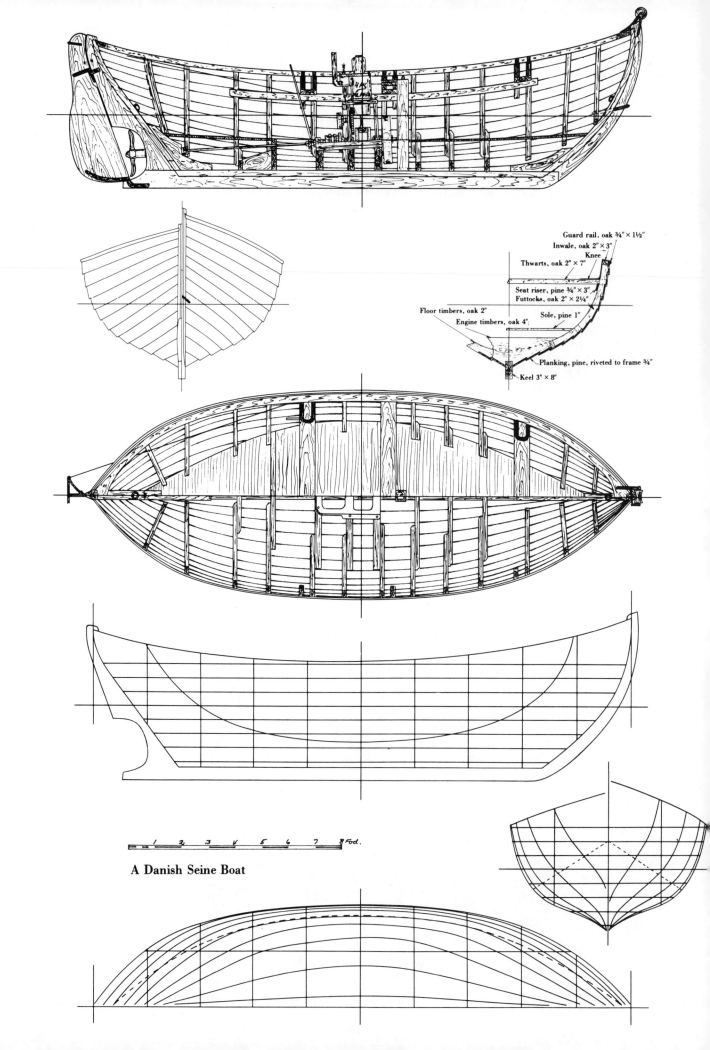

Guard rail, oak ¾″ × 1½″
Inwale, oak 2″ × 3″
Knee
Thwarts, oak 2″ × 7″
Seat riser, pine ¾″ × 3″
Futtocks, oak 2″ × 2¼″
Floor timbers, oak 2″
Sole, pine 1″
Engine timbers, oak 4″
Planking, pine, riveted to frame ¾″
Keel 3″ × 8″

A Danish Seine Boat

A Danish Seine Boat

The Danish seine boat was built at Frederikshavn around 1903. Measurement Project No. 2.
Length: 20 ft   0 in. = 6.28 m
Beam: 7 ft   3 in. = 2.28 m
Height: 3 ft 10 in. = 1.20 m
Draft: 2 ft   9 in. = 0.86 m

This is a light Danish seine boat with a motor. It was originally used as a boat to accompany one of the big cutters and was to bring the seine into place. Following the appearance of the "sharks," this boat was used to carry and set nets at the pound-net fisheries, while many other Danish seine boats were sold to fishermen in the hamlets along the North Sea coast.

When a seine was being set, the boat would have a crew of three; two men would handle the head and foot lines of the seine, while the third man would navigate. The roller at the stem was used when stones were caught in a part of the seine and it had to be lifted up and emptied.

The outside of the boat was painted white, and the gunwale and thwarts were gray. It was tarred on the inside.

An open motorboat used to set Danish seines from the bigger cutters in the background. Photograph ca. 1910.

IMPROVED COASTAL VESSELS

IT WAS NOT ONLY FREDERIKSHAVN THAT WENT IN FOR THE
new types of vessels. The North Sea coast fishermen must undoubtedly
have known that decked boats were in use at Hjerting in the 1870s and
that in 1890 there were about twenty larger boats, from nine to fourteen
tons, registered in that town. The harbors of Hjerting and Esbjerg are
well protected in comparison to the hamlets along the flat shores and
have been able to offer better anchorages for their boats. They also of-

A small cutter is seen pulling a Danish seine. The cutter has set the anchor, and the men
have used the small boat in placing the seine. The boat is seen tied to the stern of the cutter while the seine is pulled in and is emptied for the next setting. On the right, a seine is
being set from another cutter. From C. F. Drechsel: *Oversigt over vore Saltvandsfiskerier*, 1890.

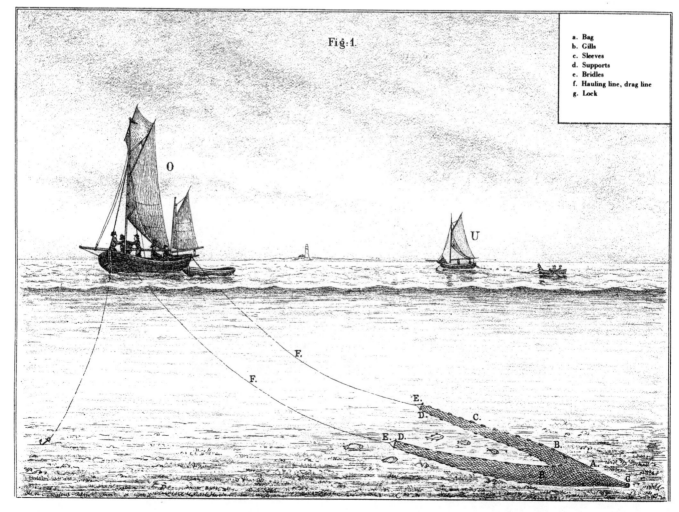

Fig. 1.

a. Bag
b. Gills
c. Sleeves
d. Supports
e. Bridles
f. Hauling line, drag line
g. Lock

fered convenient transportation via the railway out of Esbjerg. The harbor at Esbjerg, primarily intended for export of commodities, was completed in 1878, and down to 1888 the fishermen used long lines exclusively. But that year saw the introduction of the Danish seine, and after a few years the result was a considerable increase in the income of the fishermen. From 1898 on it was possible to obtain loans from the government for the purchase of fishing vessels, leading to an increase in the number of boats, and the "sharks" came to Esbjerg in 1912. While the big fisheries were being developed, fishing for home consumption continued along the coast in boats such as the pram from Hjerting.

Around 1905, the shipyards at Thisted began to build boats, similar to *Viking*, with a square stern. This development served to advance the fisheries on the west coast, and around 1915 this type of vessel began to take the place of the old Danish seine boats from Frederikshavn.

Types like *Viking* became very popular at Klitmøller and were slowly but surely adopted down along the coast, while farther north they took the place of the older Danish seine boats. Local boatbuilders improved on this type around 1930, and constructed vessels like *Bent* of Løkken, which were very wide, flat-floored keelboats. In the 1950s, these boats were spread all along the coast and are still used in the coastal fisheries with nets, trawls, and Danish seines. In the beginning, they were pulled up on shore with a hand winch, but when electric winches became common, the boats became bigger and were equipped with wheelhouses.

This development of new boat types must be viewed in the light of the flourishing of the fisheries based at Frederikshavn, Thyborøn, and Esbjerg that started right after the turn of the century. In these towns, the fishermen have for the last sixty to seventy years been able to unload their fish from their large cutters in protected harbors, while the fishermen along the coast had to unload on the open beach.

The fishing harbors at Hirtshals and Hanstenholm have since been added, but some shore fishermen still unload their fish on the rugged shores of Jutland.

Boats of the *Viking* type hauled up on the beach at Løkken. Nets and lines are drying across the masts that have been taken down. Pencil drawing by Johs. Nørretranders, 1920.

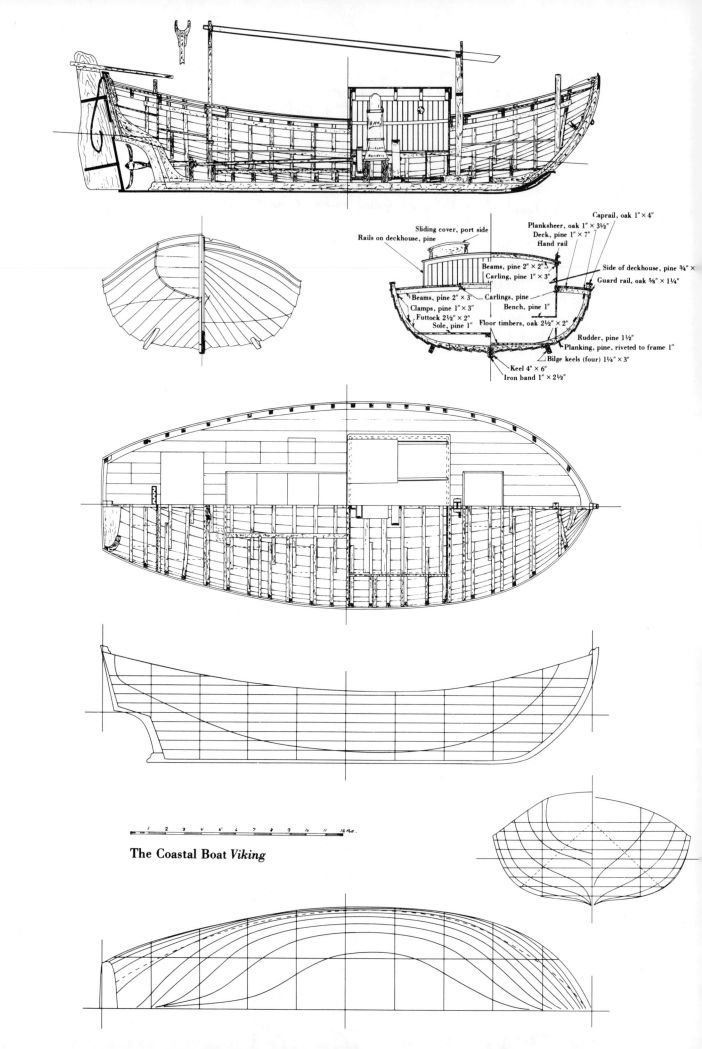

Sliding cover, port side
Rails on deckhouse, pine

Caprail, oak 1" × 4"
Planksheer, oak 1" × 3½"
Deck, pine 1" × 7"
Hand rail

Beams, pine 2" × 2"
Carling, pine 1" × 3"
Side of deckhouse, pine ¾" ×
Guard rail, oak ⅝" × 1¼"

Beams, pine 2" × 3"
Clamps, pine 1" × 3"
Futtock 2½" × 2"
Sole, pine 1"
Carlings, pine
Bench, pine 1"
Floor timbers, oak 2½" × 2"
Rudder, pine 1½"
Planking, pine, riveted to frame 1"
Bilge keels (four) 1¼" × 3"
Keel 4" × 6"
Iron band 1" × 2½"

1 2 3 4 5 6 7 8 9 10 11 12 Fod.

The Coastal Boat *Viking*

The Coastal Boat
Viking

The *Viking* of Klitmøller was built at Thisted in 1917. Measurement
Project No. 74.
Length: 27 ft 6 in. = 8.63 m
Beam: 11 ft 1 in. = 3.48 m
Height: 3 ft 9 in. = 1.18 m
Draft: ca. 3 ft 0 in. = 0.94 m

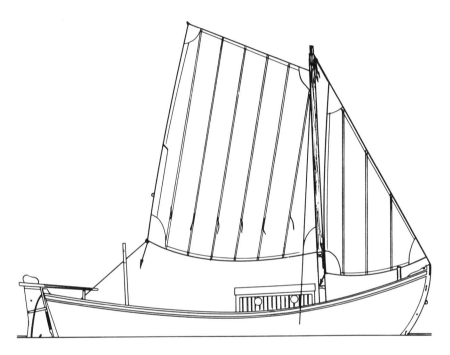

This square-sterned type with motor amidships became very popular
along Denmark's North Sea coast.

Viking was built of pine and oak and had an eight-horsepower motor.
On most boats of this type, however, the motor was later moved farther
aft, so that one could dispense with the ballast of stones and rocks they
otherwise had to carry in that area.

Viking is a predecessor of the west-coast boat that we know today,
and it took part, like the boats of today, in fishing with hook and line,
traps, and Danish seines. It had a crew of three men.

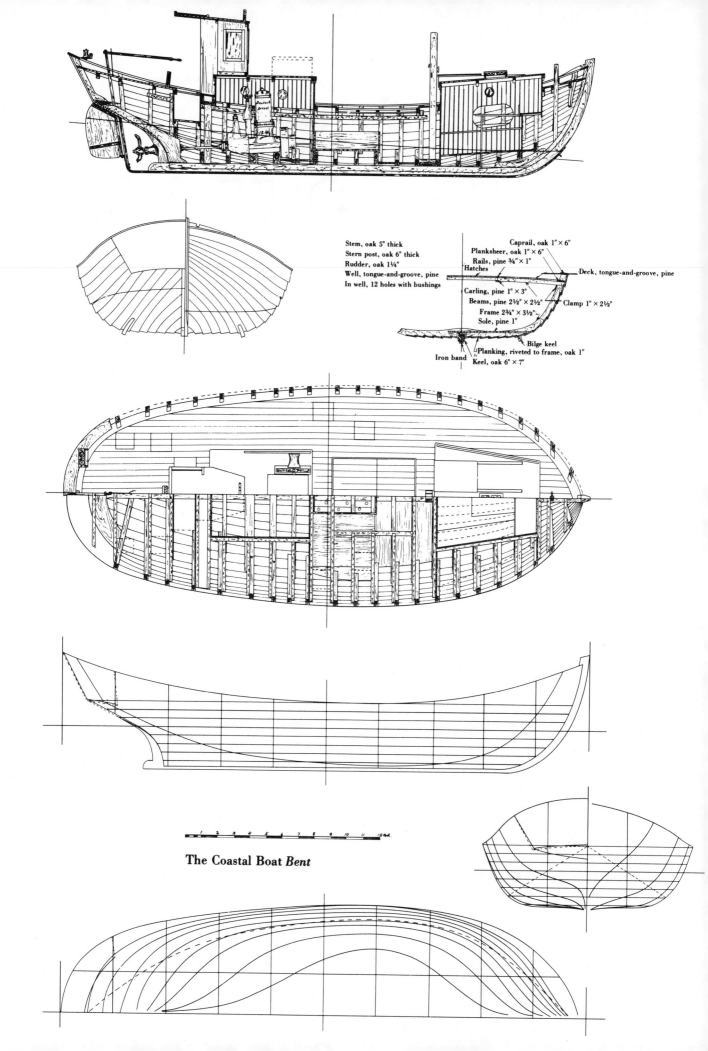

Stem, oak 5″ thick
Stern post, oak 6″ thick
Rudder, oak 1¼″
Well, tongue-and-groove, pine
In well, 12 holes with bushings

Caprail, oak 1″ × 6″
Planksheer, oak 1″ × 6″
Rails, pine ¾″ × 1″
Hatches
Deck, tongue-and-groove, pine
Carling, pine 1″ × 3″
Beams, pine 2½″ × 2½″
Clamp 1″ × 2½″
Frame 2¾″ × 3½″
Sole, pine 1″
Bilge keel
Planking, riveted to frame, oak 1″
Iron band
Keel, oak 6″ × 7″

The Coastal Boat *Bent*

The Coastal Boat
Bent

The coastal boat *Bent* of Løkken was built at North Vorupør in 1934.
Measurement Project No. 75.

Length:	32 ft 3 in. =	10.12 m
Beam:	13 ft 0 in. =	4.08 m
Height:	3 ft 10 in. =	1.20 m
Draft:	ca. 3 ft 0 in. =	0.94 m

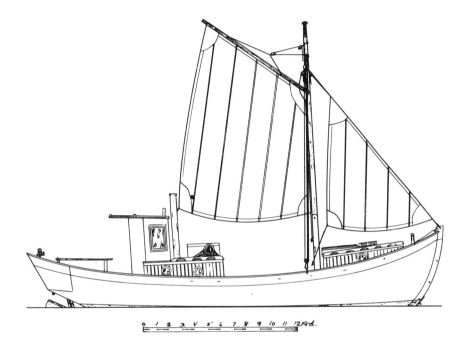

Bent is the type of coastal boat that is seen most often along Denmark's North Sea coast today. The type was introduced by boatbuilders at Klitmøller and Vorupør around 1930 as an improvement on boats such as *Viking*, and the only changes made in the current boats are the increase in their length by a few feet and a covered wheelhouse.

This boat is a very seaworthy vessel, but because of its full shape, its speed doesn't exceed six knots. It engages in the same types of fishing as does *Viking*, but during recent years most fishermen have concentrated on seining and only engage in fishing with traps and hooks and lines for the sake of the extra income that they provide. When engaged in fishing with hook and line, two of the crew, numbering three or four, take their

Bent of Løkken is being pulled up on shore. The hook is attached to an eye in the stem, and the fishermen support the boat by putting their backs to the side of the boat as it's hauled farther up on the beach. Aft, on the bulwark, are seen two seine rollers and some seine lines coiled up. The mast has been taken down in order to reduce the rolling and pitching during the fishing and the trip ashore. Photograph from around 1935.

places in the deck hatches in order to keep their balance when the boat is moving.

If the weather is favorable, this kind of fishery starts late in the night and lasts all day. The boats are put out and pulled up on the beach with the aid of an electric winch whose wire is reeved through a block that is anchored quite a distance from the shore. When returning from a day and night of fishing, the boat will be run up on the beach as far as the waves will push it before the hook of the wire is inserted in the hook on the stem and the winch is started. When putting out to sea, the boat moves stern first, but if there is an onshore wind, the boat is turned around so that the stem faces the sea.

Bent is painted in the same colors as *Viking:* the topsides are white, the bottom is red, and the bulwark is yellow. The deck and the hatch covers are varnished and the deckhouse is painted white with a green roof.

VI.
SAILING
COASTERS

THE SEA GIVES RISE TO OTHER OCCUPATIONS AND INDUS-
tries besides fishing, and of these there is no doubt that shipping and the
transportation of cargo are the most significant. Trade and commerce
presuppose that there is a certain quantity of desired goods or commodities available, that someone needs these commodities, and that they are
able to obtain them through purchase or barter. If a buyer and a seller
do not live close to each other, there has to be one more prerequisite for
such trade, namely, the fact that the commodities can be transported
from seller to buyer. In the old days, when there were no airplanes or
railroads, and the roads were few and not very good, transportation
across water was the preferred way. It would pay to send a shipment by
boat even where the sea route was much longer than overland. Shipping
is, of course, limited by the size of the vessels, the length of the sea
routes, and the conditions for loading and unloading at the ports. Also,
foreign policy, privileges, and tariff charges have interfered, although
generally only as far as ocean shipping was concerned. The smaller
cargo boats have always adhered to their own pattern, which was often
determined by geographical and social conditions.

The Danish waters are characterized by their modest depths, many
bays, sounds, and belts, which divide the country into islands and pen-
insulas. In the inner waters there are numerous natural ports, good anchorages, and the like, and even though one has to have much local
knowledge in order to be able to navigate past shallows, reefs, and sandbars, one must admit that the Danish waters are a favorable area for
sailing and navigation. In addition, flatners used to navigate on some
small rivers and streams, and this mode of transportation was also common in the tidal flats.

There are extensive tidal flats off the southern part of Denmark's
North Sea coast; it is a very shallow sea with many islands and with
sand and mudbanks that dry out at ebb tide. It would be impossible for

normal keelboats to sail along these coasts, and in the eighteenth century almost the only boats to be seen in this region were hoys, smacks, *kuffs*, and *everts* (sailing barges), types of vessels that were common in Germany and Holland, where there are large coastal areas of the same character.

The type of vessel that has been in use the longest is the sailing barge (*evert*), a flat-bottomed vessel with a square stern and ten to forty tons in size. It was not very costly to build, and at high tide it could enter the tidal flats and pull up its leeboards to just rest on the bottom. These sailing barges carried most of the cargo to and from the Danish islands in the North Sea, including timber, stones and rocks, fuel, and everything else the islanders needed. The most common type of freight, however, was hay from the marshlands. The shipments between the hamlets on the mainland consisted mainly of general cargo, building materials, and coal.

The vessels used not only the harbors to load and unload, but just as often the very beach, where the sailing barge could run in at high tide and load at ebb tide in just a few inches of water. The loading was done from a horse-drawn wagon or a wheelbarrow, which was pulled up alongside the boat. Transportation with sailing barges continued far into the present century, until they were completely superseded by trucks and ferries.

The sloop (*jagt*) is another well-known vessel that has been widely used for centuries in the Danish inner waters and also in the North Sea and the Baltic.

A sailing barge (*evert*) loading hay from a horse-drawn wagon driven by the two women on shore. The boat is resting on the bottom in the shallow water. The stripes along the boat's hull are clearly seen. In the background, fishermen are catching eel in nets. The place shown is probably Nordby on the island of Fanø. Color lithograph by Christian Blache, 1883.

In the second half of the seventeenth century there were many types of small vessels, of which the sloop was the one which became most popular during the following hundred years. During the 1700s there were two types of sloops. One type had a vertical stem and very concave lines to the hull, and the other was the sloop with a square stern, curved stem, and great sheer. The latter type, which *inter alia* was less expensive to build, became the most popular one. Sloops such as *De fire Brødre* of Marstal carried a great deal of the cargo transported in Scandinavian waters. Most of the boats were registered in towns that had the privilege to conduct maritime trade and transport, but in actuality they had to compete with ships from other villages and fishing hamlets. Thus, the town of Ærøskøbing often complained about the lively trade carried out by the citizens of the village of Marstal with the southern islands and with Schleswig and Holstein.

Marstal in the 1700s arranged for a large number of shipments of grain and pork from the islands of Lolland and Fyn to Copenhagen. However, the flourishing state of the town received a blow during the war with England in 1807–1814, during which Denmark was allied with Napoleonic France; much of the trade came to a complete stop and many ships were captured by the English. In addition, a great number of houses burned in 1815, but the people of Marstal worked energetically to open new lanes of commerce and trade, and the town's fleet of sailing ships grew apace. In 1864, the island of Ærø became a part of Denmark instead of, as previously, belonging to the duchies, and a beginning was made of building bigger ships than the traditional sloops. Even though competition with the steamships ensued, the fleet of ketches, schooners, and barkentines continued to grow and the jointly owned shipping firms of Ærø managed for many years to obtain cargoes for their sailing ships that the steamships didn't want to handle, including cargoes of lumber from the Gulf of Bothnia, dried fish from Newfoundland, hides, sugar, or, once in a great while, saltpeter from South America. Following a number of depression periods, however, many sailing-ship owners had to give up, and the ships were sold in great numbers, to be used mostly in local trade with auxiliary motors installed.

There were only a few coastal towns that developed on the scale of Marstal. Only a few ships were registered in most towns, the majority of them not being owned by a shipping company but by the skipper himself. He was thus in complete control of what cargoes he wanted to accept, often being able to secure new cargoes under way. Because of the small size of the vessels and the haphazard way the cargoes were obtained, the skippers had to contend with poor and risky conditions when loading and unloading.

The sloop *Anna* of Vejle (ex-*De fire Brødre* of Marstal) photographed from the end of the jibboom. In the foreground are seen the windlass and bitts; amidships, the two owners are working the winch; aft, on the quarterdeck, on the starboard side, is seen the companion to the cabin. An eel spear is lying on the port side of the deck; in a dead calm such a spear might provide the crew with a free dinner. Photograph from 1939.

During the last century there was a lively traffic with sloops from the west coast of northern Jutland to the southern part of Norway. The ships sailed north with butter, grain, and pork, and brought timber back with them. Since there were no protected anchorages or harbors along the coast of North Jutland, the vessels had to anchor very close to shore and hope that the sea would not become so turbulent that they were driven up on the beach. Since deep-draft vessels were also used in this trade, they could not be run right up on the beach, unless their bottoms had been reinforced or specially built for this rough treatment. The vessels that had been built with the trade with Norway in mind were called sand boats because of their means of loading and unloading.

Since the draft of the ordinary sloops was rather considerable for their size, they could not be run up on the beach; nor could one drive a wagon out to where they were lying. It was therefore necessary to have a small boat carry the cargo out to the sloop. Large, low, wide flat-bottomed barges, called flatboats, were used for this purpose. Each barge belonged to the harbor or village in question and was also used by a salvage association when unloading cargo if a ship that had run aground had to be made lighter to float. The flatboats were rowed back and forth between the beach and the ship until the latter was fully loaded, whereupon they were hauled up on the beach. In the wintertime they would often be housed in a shed.

In regard to the trade with Norway, several hamlets built it up to such an extent that merchants often had large warehouses built, as, for example, the "butter-merchant's warehouse" at Løkken. The merchants would often be the owners of their ships and hired a skipper to command them, but it might also happen that the owners were farmers in the neighborhood.

The traffic with barges (called *Kåg*) on Denmark's many bays and

A flatner on the river Gudenå. The cargo consists of bricks. A young helper stands at the stem, busily trying to keep the vessel away from the shore. Painting by Rasmus Christiansen, 1894.

rivers goes far back in time. One example is the traffic on the river Gudenå, on which almost 120 barges were in service around 1860. Some of them were still there at the end of World War II, but they have since been replaced by trucks. The Randers barges were very long, flat-bottomed, and narrow vessels with a ring deck and a small deckhouse for the crew.

The barges were used in all kinds of transport on the river, carrying, for instance, bricks, fuel, pulp, hay, and peat.

When the wind and current were favorable, they carried sails, but when the current ran the other way the barges had to be poled or pulled up the river by men who made a specialty of such a task. They were not a part of the crew and were not allowed to enter the little cabin. These bargemen were paid by the day and were ill-treated. The boats would, as one would expect, run aground on sandbanks, and the like, in the river. In such cases the bargemen would drive a special hand winch into the sandy shore and would work it with handspikes after a hawser from the barge had been made fast to the winch. When the boat had been floated again, the winch and other equipment were stowed away and the trip was continued.

The fjord barges carried not only goods destined for places on the fjord but just as frequently brought cargoes to hamlets on the coast near the mouth of the fjord, from where the cargoes were transported on smaller boats. Even small sloops and ketches might have difficulty in negotiating the shallow fjords, and therefore until more recent times they had to have their cargoes transported by barges as far as the mouths of the fjords.

Danish coastal vessels handled these transshipments for many years, but cutters and sloops became a part of the picture at the middle of the nineteenth century. These were boats that had less sheer and ornamentation than the picturesque Danish sloops. Since many of the new vessels were fine sailers, the new styles were adopted by the Danish boatbuilders. The famous boatwright E. C. Benzon of Nykøbing Falster in 1867 built the first of a new type of sloop and called it *Castor*. *Castor* was quite different from the old type of sloop. It had slimmer lines, and its mast and bowsprit were each made of one piece of timber. The sheer had been greatly modified and moldings and ornamentation had been left out. *Castor* was a fine sailer, at times outdistancing faster and more elegant custom sloops. It was placed in the packet service with general cargo from the southern parts of Denmark to Copenhagen. It had a crew of three men, who also handled the loading and unloading of the cargo. E. C. Benzon was a skillful boatbuilder who made frequent use of drawings, a practice not very common as far as the building of smaller vessels for the merchant marine was concerned. He supplied, for instance, the drawings to shipwrights at Marstal who, even at the end of the 1800s, continued to build in the old-fashioned way.

The new type of sloop spread to many parts of the country, and many sloops were later lengthened and rerigged as ketches. They continued to build these small coastal ships until the 1920s and in some places even as late as World War II. On the island of Ærø boatbuilders met the demand for bigger boats in the maritime trade by building schooners and barkentines with heart-shaped sterns and curved stems on the model of the small sloops and ketches.

At the time that sails were on the wane as a means of propulsion, and the yards changed over to building steel ships or making wooden cutters, the sloops and ketches continued to carry general domestic cargo with only two changes, namely that they now had had engines installed and the crew had been reduced from three to two (or even, at times, the skipper alone). The fate of the schooners, however, was different. They were called home from the more substantial foreign trades when steam and motor ships had replaced them on their last profitable routes. So many of the ports had by then been so much improved that sailing ships were not the only ones that dared enter them. The jointly owned shipping firms sold the schooners to Sweden, where they could bring in a sufficient income for some years because of the different rules pertaining to ownership. Many of the schooners were also sold to individual skippers, who, as shipowners, carried on packet and general cargo services among Denmark's many islands.

Thus, the schooners, which had been built for entirely different purposes, ended their freight-carrying days in the same trade as the small sloops, which over a hundred years earlier had been their model for building. A few of these small boats are still sailing, manned with the "smallholders of the sea," but their operation becomes less and less profitable because of the increased costs, and the price of these ships dropped considerably at the beginning of the 1960s. Their prices have risen again during the last few years because of the growing interest on the part of those who buy the ships to convert into pleasure craft.

The packet ship *Zeus*, built in 1876 by the boatbuilder E. C. Benzon. The vessel, which in the picture is carrying much cargo on deck, sailed for many years on a route between Copenhagen and Nykøbing Falster. Photograph from Guldborgsund, taken ca. 1900.

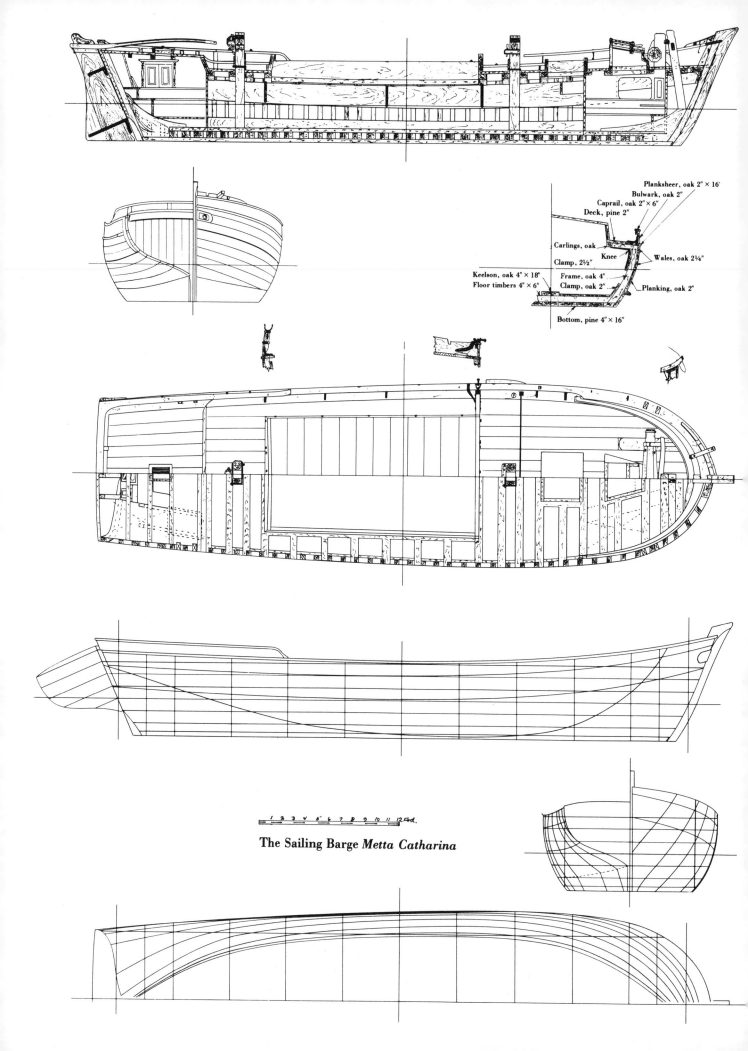

Plankster, oak 2" × 16'
Bulwark, oak 2"
Caprail, oak 2" × 6"
Deck, pine 2"

Carlings, oak
Knee
Clamp, 2½"
Wales, oak 2¼"

Keelson, oak 4" × 18"
Floor timbers 4" × 6"
Frame, oak 4"
Clamp, oak 2"
Planking, oak 2"

Bottom, pine 4" × 16"

1 2 3 4 5 6 7 8 9 10 11 12Ftd.

The Sailing Barge *Metta Catharina*

The Sailing Barge
Metta Catharina

The *Metta Catharina* was built at Haseldorf, Germany, in 1904. Measurement Project No. 34.

Length: 48 ft 3 in. = 15.14 m
Beam: 14 ft 6 in. = 4.55 m
Height: 5 ft 2 in. = 1.62 m
Draft without
    leeboard: 3 ft 0 in. = 0.94 m
Draft with
    leeboard: 7 ft 9 in. = 2.43 m

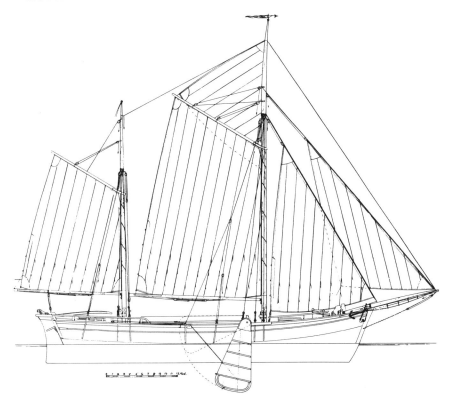

This sailing barge, which in 1920 was sold to new owners at Nakskov, is a powerful, carvel-built vessel with a completely flat bottom. The topside planking is oak, while the bottom is pine. Two leeboards are fitted amidships, one on each side, and are used while under way to prevent drifting. The garboard plank on each side is very wide and acts as a longitudinal strengthening element.

Metta Catharina is rigged as a ketch and has been used as a cargo ship and to fish up boulders from the bottom of the sea. Aft, there is a small cabin for the skipper, and forward there is a cabin for the crew.

The outside of the hull and the leeboards were tarred black, and the wale, the stern, the planksheer, and the gunwale were scraped bright and gleaming. Moldings, hawseholes, and anchor-handling gear were white, and the cabin, coamings, the inside of the bulwark as well as mast collars and booms were painted light green. The masts were black, with white tops.

Two-masted sailing barge at Wedel at the mouth of the Elbe. Drawing by Friedrich Peters-Weben, ca. 1912.

The Sloop
De Fire Brødre

De Fire Brødre of Marstal was built by H. C. Friis at Marstal in 1794.
Measurement Project No. 31.
Length: 44 ft 2 in. = 13.86 m
Beam: 13 ft 2 in. = 4.13 m
Height: 7 ft 8 in. = 2.41 m
Draft: ca. 5 ft 0 in. = 1.57 m

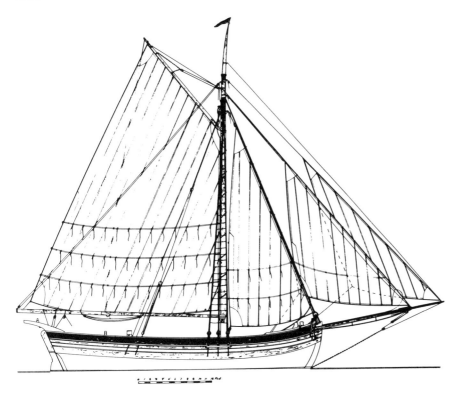

During its 150 years, this sloop was altered very little. A motor was
never installed; the only changes are the somewhat larger hatches and
winches, a different windlass, and a new mast. It retained to the last its
decorative stripes along the sides and continued to carry freight until
1943, when it was wrecked at Strib under the name *Anna* of Vejle.
   The sloop was a powerful carvel-built vessel with a rather bluff bow.
All but its decks and bulwarks were oak (those being pine). The bowsprit was on the port side of the stem and the jibboom on the starboard
side. Two wooden rosettes were placed on the stern with leaf orna-

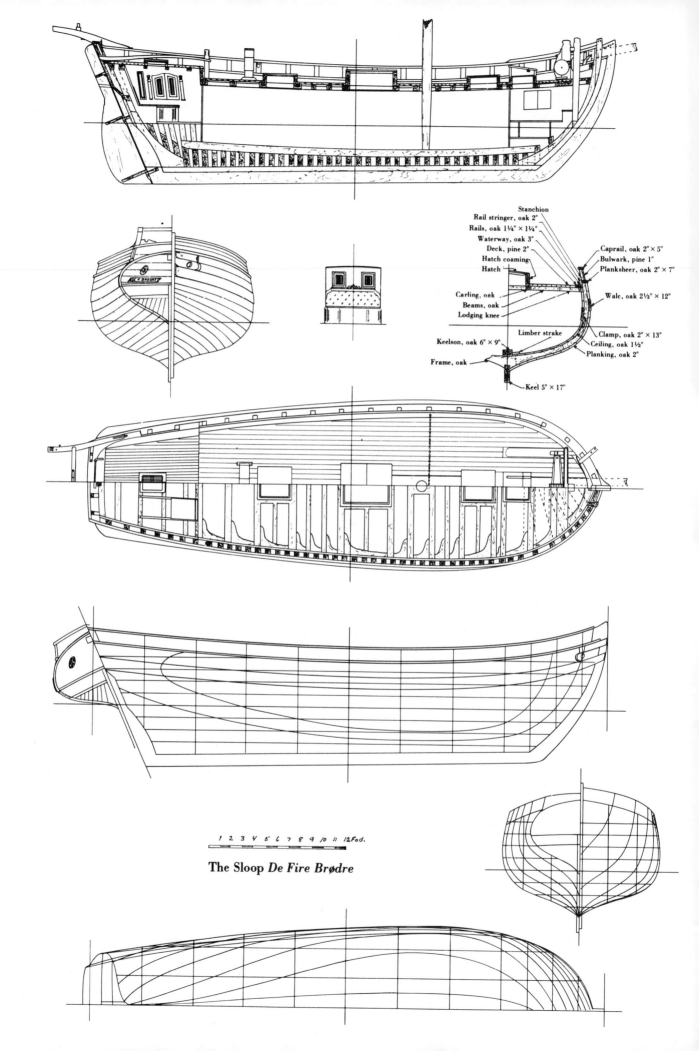

Stanchion
Rail stringer, oak 2″
Rails, oak 1¼″ × 1¼″
Waterway, oak 3″
Deck, pine 2″
Hatch coaming
Hatch

Caprail, oak 2″ × 5″
Bulwark, pine 1″
Planksheer, oak 2″ × 7″

Carling, oak
Beams, oak
Lodging knee

Wale, oak 2½″ × 12″

Limber strake

Clamp, oak 2″ × 13″
Ceiling, oak 1½″
Planking, oak 2″

Keelson, oak 6″ × 9″

Frame, oak

Keel 5″ × 17″

1 2 3 4 5 6 7 8 9 10 11 12 Fod.

The Sloop *De Fire Brødre*

The sloop *Anna* photographed a few years before it was wrecked in 1943. The bowsprit and the jibboom, which are attached on either side of the stem, are clearly seen, and the decorative stripes along the hull accentuate the sheer of the vessel.

ments that were painted white. The sloop would usually sail between the Danish islands. The crew consisted of a skipper and one boy.

The vessel was painted white below, and the topsides as far as the wale were painted yellow. Then came the decorative stripes in white, brown, and green. The planksheer was red, the bulwark was black, and the gunwale was gray. The booms were painted white, the rigging was black, the bowsprit and jibboom green.

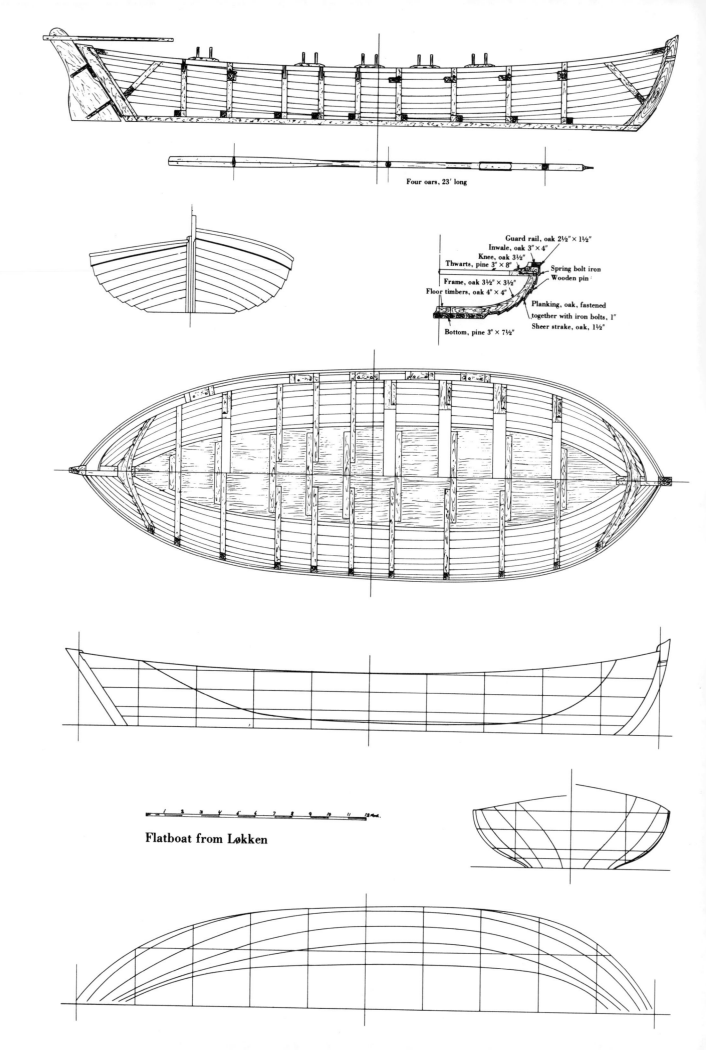

Four oars, 23' long

Guard rail, oak 2½" × 1½"
Inwale, oak 3" × 4"
Knee, oak 3½"
Thwarts, pine 3" × 8"
Spring bolt iron
Wooden pin
Frame, oak 3½" × 3½"
Floor timbers, oak 4" × 4"
Planking, oak, fastened
together with iron bolts, 1"
Sheer strake, oak, 1½"
Bottom, pine 3" × 7½"

Flatboat from Løkken

Flatboat from Løkken

This flatboat was built in Lyngby around 1890. Measurement Project
No. 70.
Length: 31 ft   6 in. = 9.89 m
Beam: 10 ft 10 in. = 3.40 m
Height: 3 ft   0 in. = 0.94 m
Draft: ca. 1 ft   0 in. = 0.31 m

This boat has a completely flat pine bottom, while its planks and ribs are
made of oak. Special bolts reinforce the connection between the planking and the thwarts, in order to prevent the sides from bulging outward
on account of the heavy cargo.

The flatboat was engaged in loading and unloading bigger ships and
was useful in aiding ships that had run aground. When a ship was to be
pulled or warped off a shoal, the flatboat would take the ship's ground
tackle on board, and with the big anchor hanging from its gunwale, it
was rowed out to a suitable spot for the swinging of the ship, where it
then dropped the anchor. Then the boat would return to the ship and
take on board as much cargo as possible, which would then be unloaded
on the beach.

This procedure was repeated until they knew that the ship would be
floating at high tide. When the ship was once again in deep water, the
cargo was returned to the ship.

When a ship was warped off a shoal, a full crew would row the flatboat with the ship in tow. All oars were used at the same time, but the
foremost and aftermost pairs of oars were not in the water at the same
time, since the boat had to be subjected every second to the force driv-
ing it forward in order to be able to pull the heavy cable. As the boat
moved across the shallow bottom, the anchor chain was paid out over
the stern of the stranded vessel.

The flatboat was coated with tar on the outside and the inside, with
the exception of the gunwale and parts of the thwarts, which were
painted white.

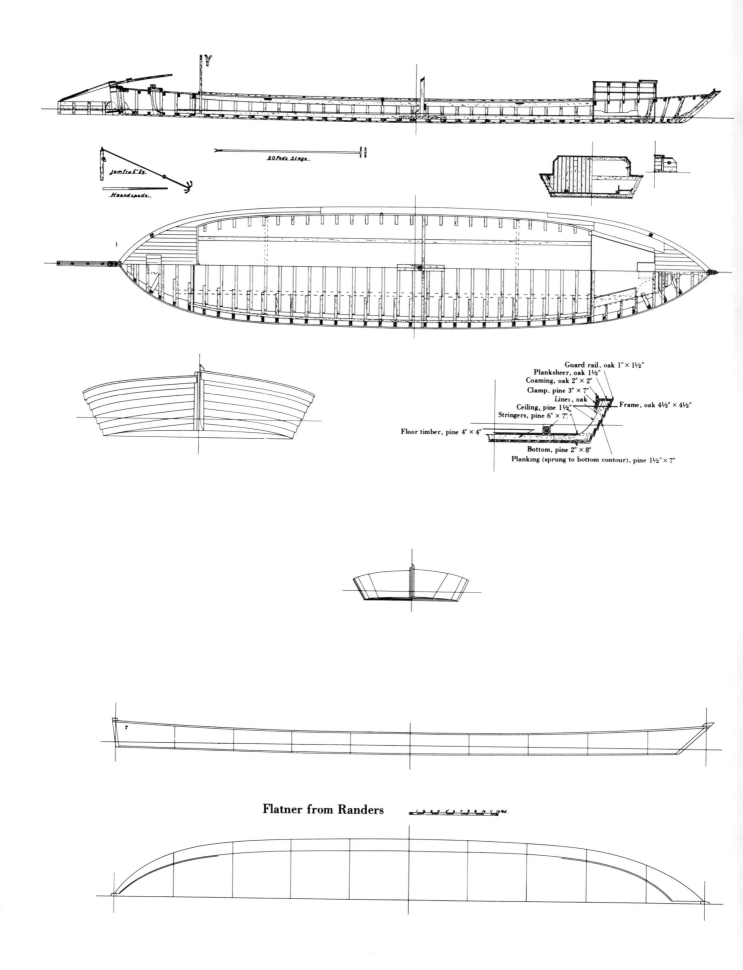

Guard rail, oak 1" × 1½"
Planksheer, oak 1½"
Coaming, oak 2" × 2"
Clamp, pine 3" × 7"
Liner, oak
Ceiling, pine 1½"
Stringers, pine 6" × 7"
Floor timber, pine 4" × 4"
Frame, oak 4½" × 4½"
Bottom, pine 2" × 8"
Planking (sprung to bottom contour), pine 1½" × 7"

Flatner from Randers

Flatner from Randers

This flatner was built at Randers in 1917–1918. Measurement Project No. 35.

Length: 80 ft 0 in. = 25.11 m
Beam: 15 ft 8 in. = 4.92 m
Height: 2 ft 9 in. = 0.86 m
Draft: ca. 1 ft 2 in. = 0.37 m

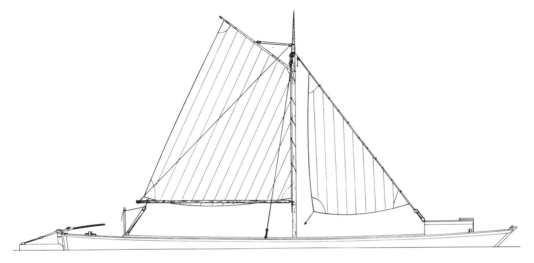

This flatner (*kåg*) is a very slender vessel; like many of the Gudenå flat-ners, it was built by a house carpenter. The hull is made of pine and oak and the flat bottom is of pine. The flatner was used exclusively for transporting various commodities. Because of the shallow water, the rudder was shallow and wide.

The flatner was tarred, except for the deckhouse, which was painted.

Flatner on the river Gudenå. A fully loaded flatner is being pulled up the river by a team of horses, while a man with a long pole at the stem makes certain that the boat will not hit the riverbank. In the background, another flatner sailing in the opposite direction. Drawing by Hans Smidt in M. Galschiøt: *Danmark*, 1887.

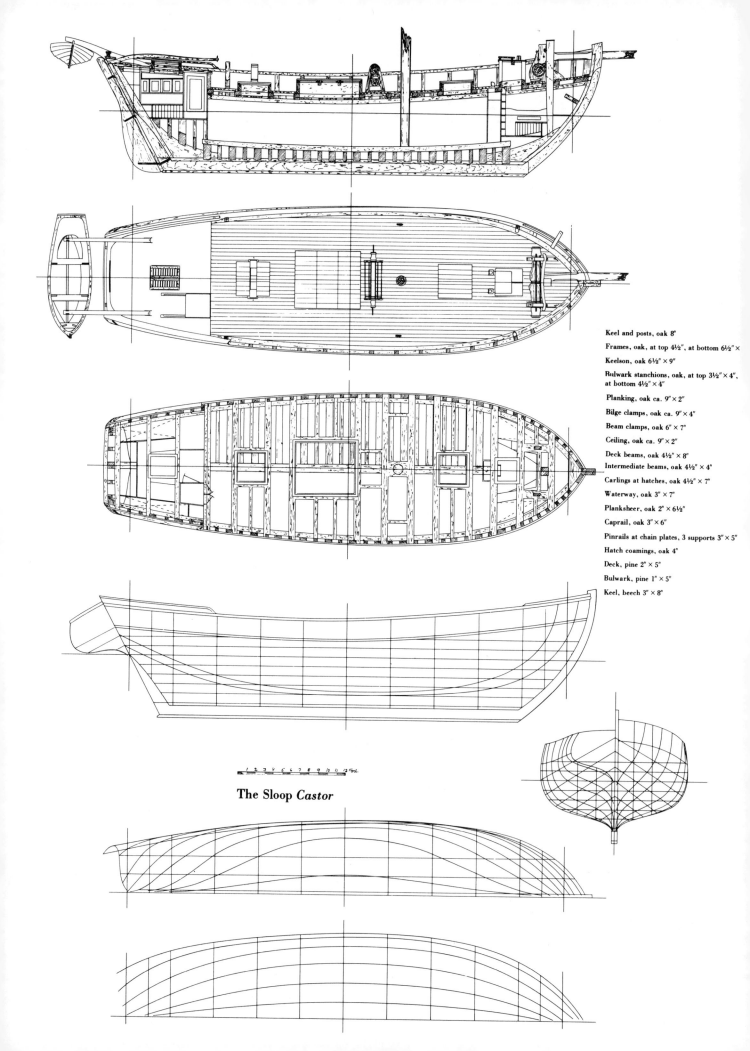

Keel and posts, oak 8″

Frames, oak, at top 4½″, at bottom 6½″ ×

Keelson, oak 6½″ × 9″

Bulwark stanchions, oak, at top 3½″ × 4″,
at bottom 4½″ × 4″

Planking, oak ca. 9″ × 2″

Bilge clamps, oak ca. 9″ × 4″

Beam clamps, oak 6″ × 7″

Ceiling, oak ca. 9″ × 2″

Deck beams, oak 4½″ × 8″

Intermediate beams, oak 4½″ × 4″

Carlings at hatches, oak 4½″ × 7″

Waterway, oak 3″ × 7″

Planksheer, oak 2″ × 6½″

Caprail, oak 3″ × 6″

Pinrails at chain plates, 3 supports 3″ × 5″

Hatch coamings, oak 4″

Deck, pine 2″ × 5″

Bulwark, pine 1″ × 5″

Keel, beech 3″ × 8″

The Sloop *Castor*

The Sloop *Castor*

The sloop *Castor* was built by shipbuilder E. C. Benzon at Nykøbing
Falster in 1867. Measurement Project No. 32.

Length: 48 ft 0 in. = 15.06 m
Beam: 16 ft 0 in. = 5.02 m
Depth from the
   bottom of the
   rabbet to the
   planksheer: 7 ft 0 in. = 2.20 m
Draft: ca. 6 ft 6 in. = 2.04 m
Tonnage: 32.16 gross tons

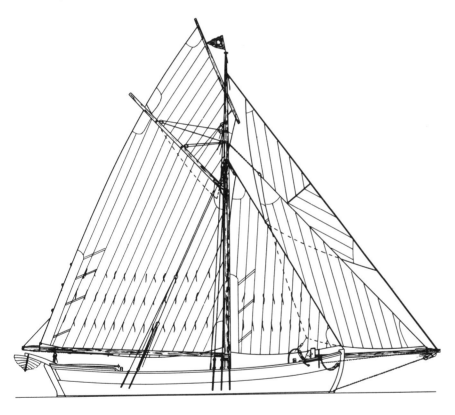

Castor is a carvel-built sloop with a heart-shaped stern and convex
stem. The vessel, which was intended for the packet trade, was built of
oak, with ribs set on ten-inch centers. The beam shelf, which supports
the wide deck beams, was about square and was cut to shape before being
put in place. This was one of shipbuilder Benzon's patents, because he

The sloop *Castor* moored at the Bourse in Copenhagen. The sails are bent on, and the light boom, or whisker pole, of the flying jib is rigged upward toward the masthead. The picture was taken during *Castor*'s last packet trip as a pure sailing ship, prior to a motor being installed in 1921. It was made longer and was rerigged as a ketch in 1926.

discovered that the primary task of the beam shelf was to strengthen the ship athwartships and not exclusively to support the beams. *Castor,* which was well furnished with vertical knees, was otherwise a lightly built vessel, which added to its cargo-carrying capacity.

The skipper had his cabin aft, while the crew, consisting of a seaman and a boy, slept forward. *Castor* had a rather high bulwark for its size, since the packet trade demanded space for such deck cargo as bales and barrels.

The vessel's bottom had been coated with a copper compound; it was painted black with a white stripe along the bulwark. The gunwale was brown with white anchor catheads. Interior supports, the bulwark, binnacle, companion bitts, and pawl bitt were painted light green, as was the interior of the stern dinghy, whose exterior was black.

VII.
SERVICE BOATS

WHENEVER A BUSINESS OR ACTIVITY GROWS IN SIZE, IT WILL be in need of certain services, which, due to fluctuations in demand, may often be too costly for the business itself to institute and to support. Organizations as well as individuals have looked upon this as an opportunity to obtain extra income, and there are many who have met these varying demands and have seen their activities become established occupations. Such occupations are called service trades. Within civilian maritime affairs there have been a number of trades and crafts besides the pilot service, the activities of bumboatmen, and the iceboat service. Regulations concerning commerce and tariffs led to opportunities for smuggling, and in order to enforce its customs regulations the state in the early 1700s established its maritime customs inspectorate.

In 1818, at the end of the war with England, the Customs Department obtained seven revenue cutters in order to combat smuggling. The boats were stationed in different strategically important areas and were to cruise under the command of naval officers in the Danish sounds and belts as well as the waters off Schleswig and Holstein.

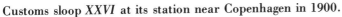
Customs sloop *XXVI* at its station near Copenhagen in 1900.

Ships that were destined for Danish or Norwegian ports, when boarded by men from the revenue cutters, were obliged to show their papers to the commanding officer, who had the right, if he found it necessary, to bring the ship to a royal customhouse for further inspection. New regulations were instituted in 1824, at which time the maritime customs service was reorganized, but no important changes were added down to the dissolution of the service in 1904.

These customs sloops had to be swift ships and easy to maneuver. The boats used to have square sterns, but in 1853 E. C. Benzon supplied the Ministry of Finance with the first sharp-sterned customs sloop. This sloop was well suited to its task, and N. F. Hansen of Odense built several vessels of this type for the Customs Service. The number of sloops varied, but there were, as a rule, between thirty and forty-five vessels on the alert. Aside from the Customs Service, each station was obliged to give information to the Meteorological Institute, to provide guidance and assistance to other ships, to provide help when a vessel was shipwrecked, to help the life-saving service, and to aid in the transportation of pastors and physicians. Besides the customs assistant, the crew consisted of the skipper or, as he was called, the police officer, who had a chief officer's license, a few able seamen, and a boy.

These customs sloops were indeed able to inspect a considerable number of ships. In 1896, for instance, no less than 19,069 vessels were boarded.

The Customs Service was far from being a beloved organization; the steamships especially complained about being delayed by boardings. At the end of the 1800s it was thought that the system was out-of-date, and following many complaints from the shipowners, in 1899 it was made unlawful to board the ships, and the sloops had only one task left, that of patrolling the coasts. The number of sloops was greatly reduced, and the customs maritime cruiser service was disbanded in 1904. The remaining crew members obtained other work or were hired for some of the newly established jobs, such as controllers or customs assistants. The Customs Service was not without ships for very long, however. The need to control smuggling soon became evident, and in 1920 four new customs cutters once again plied the waves, but this time they were of a somewhat different construction and were supplied with powerful motors.

In order for the big vessels to pass unharmed through the inner Danish waters, they often needed the assistance of people with knowledge of the local conditions and able to help with the navigation. The ships might ask a fisherman to act as an amateur pilot, but this task was, in time, made into a real occupation, and private pilot stations were established with definite duties and government charters. Several pilot stations were established in the seventeenth century, and in certain areas the ships were compelled to take on pilots, a practice that gave the pilots a very handsome income. Either the pilots would be the owners of their boats or the boats were owned by the pilot station. In the old days, the boats were always of the open type; among the southern Danish islands the boats would be spritsail-rigged with two or three masts, but in the Belts the boats would have one mast with a spritsail or a gaffsail.

Such were also the boats of the Helsingør pilots until the middle of the 1860s, when the pilot station built two new pilot boats, whose names were *Esbern Snare* and *Helsingør*. They were both rather large, decked vessels, the latter being in reality a Sound boat that had been adapted to the special requirements of piloting. *Esbern Snare*, which had been built somewhat earlier by E. C. Benzon at Nykøbing, was designed to be something entirely new as far as pilot boats were concerned, but the interesting thing was that the two boats, aside from Benzon's high bulwark and tall mast, resembled each other to a very high degree, which no doubt was due to the high level reached by the boatbuilders on the Sound.

When there were several pilots attached to the same station, they would take turns looking for ships signaling for a pilot. There were, of course, places where the conditions were more undisciplined and where

The pilot boat *Helsingør* in the harbor of Helsingør, lying behind Svitzer's steamship *Drogden*. There is a diver's pump on board *Helsingør*, and on its starboard side one can clearly see the big fenders. Photograph from the 1890s.

the different pilots would race out to the ships in order to get the job. While waiting for a pilot, the ship would be braced aback, but when the pilot was on board, the ship would proceed through the difficult waters under his full command and responsibility. Some pilots would have their boats taken in tow by the ship, while others were merely put on board and had them sailed back to the station. When the ship had paid off the pilot, he either had to get passage back to his home or be put ashore and take care of transportation in some other way, unless he was fortunate enough to meet with a ship that needed a pilot for a voyage in the opposite direction. The pilots usually still work in this manner, and they still own their boats.

The two pilot boats at Helsingør later had motors installed and were sold in the mid-1930s when the pilot station obtained its first real motor pilot boat, which is still in use when there is a need for an extra boat.

The bigger sailing ships and steamships setting out for foreign ports might spend a long time before reaching their destinations. Some of the food might give out, making it very convenient to have one's supplies replenished in the Sound, as on a voyage, for instance, from an Atlantic or North Sea port to the Baltic. Before the days of frozen food, the crews would, for the most part, eat salted fare, and when all or most of it was consumed, the skipper was in the market for new provisions. Only seldom, however, did the skipper buy fresh meat, even if it were available, since salted meat was less expensive and would be edible for a much longer time. There was also a need to contact the shore in order to obtain cloth, tobacco, knives, and soap. Not only the skipper and the mates did some shopping—the crew members, too, would purchase things on the sly, if they had any ready money on them.

Since the ships did not enter any of the harbors, the suppliers had to do their business with the ship while it lay at anchor or was sailing through the Sound. Many fishermen would take care of this commerce, either as independent entrepreneurs or in partnership with a merchant. The fisherman would fill his boat with the commodities for which he thought there would be a demand, such as fresh-baked bread, potatoes, and vegetables, and would sail out to the passing ship. There would be haggling about the prices and the quality of the goods, and the fisherman would, of course, prefer to receive ready cash in payment. But very often he would be offered various kinds of products, especially if the ship was returning from the tropics or other warm climes, and a barter session would ensue.

This form of trade was called bumming. Many fishermen left fishing behind in the summertime in order to make a living as bumboatmen. Special dinghies were built for this purpose, and many merchants established firms specializing in bumming. The need for this kind of trade disappeared, however, when the ships became faster and were equipped with refrigerators. But chance transactions with passing ships have occurred off and on down to this very day; from the hamlet Sletten on the Sound, for example.

The transport of persons, cargo, and mail across the Belts has long been rather well organized. To the passengers, the trips were not very comfortable, but the more important junctions for ferries and for the mails were placed under state control early on, the result being improved service. A great number of small mail routes between the southern islands were still being serviced by smallholders and fishermen in tiny dinghies, but at the big ferry harbors in between the stagecoach stopovers, regular service was established with mail sloops and other smaller ships—provided the weather was favorable. If the wind was unfavorable, the crossing of the Great Belt might take several days, and in the winter the Belt might freeze over so that it was impossible to cross by boat. In such cases, travelers might want to resort to iceboats.

These iceboats were rowing or sailing vessels, which had been equipped with sledge runners, so that they could be pulled across the ice without being damaged. When they came to open water, the boat was put into the water and the trip was continued with sails or oars until frozen ice was again encountered. The crew of such an iceboat consisted of five or six men, who worked as day laborers in this trade. The post office and later the national railways owned some of these iceboats, which often, in winter, formed long processions across the Belts. Iceboats were also used by the pilot stations, if the ice became too strong for their own pilot boats to force.

Since the introduction of the icebreakers and the powerful motor ferries, this kind of journey across the ice is no longer necessary, but in some places they still have an old-fashioned iceboat available, as, for instance, at the Dragør pilot station. It may be used if the cold is so great that the icebreaker is not able to keep a channel open in the ice for the pilot boats.

Iceboats at Halsskov Reef. In the background is seen the newly arrived train. On the left is the signal station. Photograph from 1898.

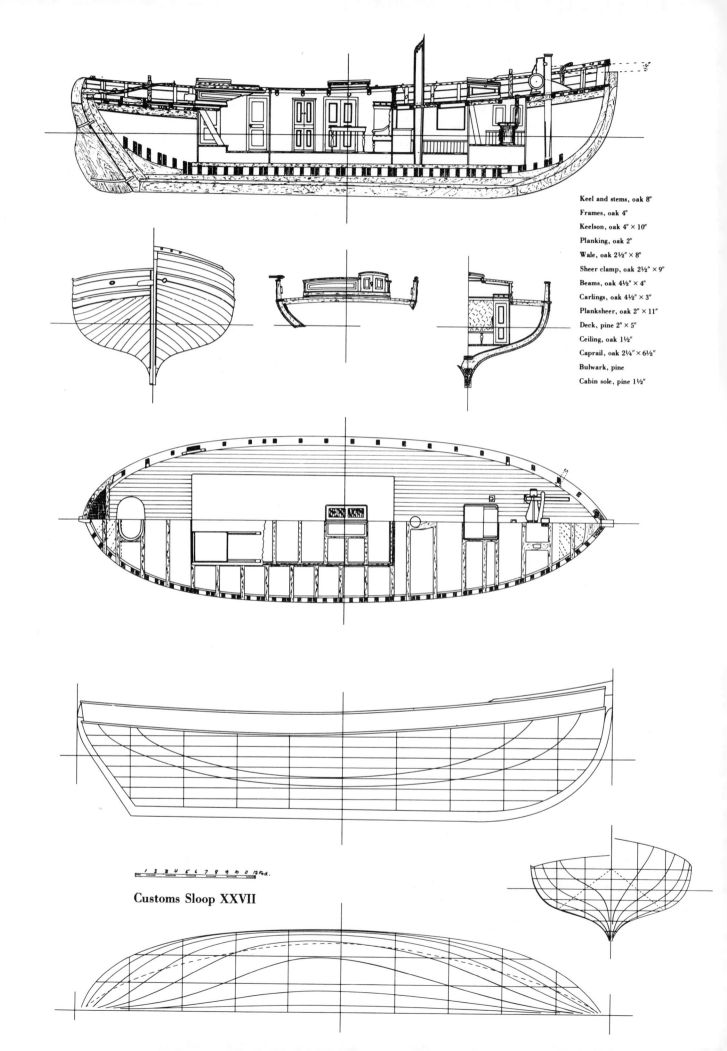

Keel and stems, oak 8″

Frames, oak 4″

Keelson, oak 4″ × 10″

Planking, oak 2″

Wale, oak 2½″ × 8″

Sheer clamp, oak 2½″ × 9″

Beams, oak 4½″ × 4″

Carlings, oak 4½″ × 3″

Planksheer, oak 2″ × 11″

Deck, pine 2″ × 5″

Ceiling, oak 1½″

Caprail, oak 2¼″ × 6½″

Bulwark, pine

Cabin sole, pine 1½″

Customs Sloop XXVII

Customs Sloop *XXVII*

This customs sloop was built by the shipbuilder N. F. Hansen in Odense
in 1890. Measurement Project No. 33.
Length: 52 ft   6 in. = 16.48 m
Beam: 15 ft   8 in. = 4.92 m
Height: 6 ft 11 in. = 2.17 m
Draft: ca. 6 ft   0 in. = 1.88 m

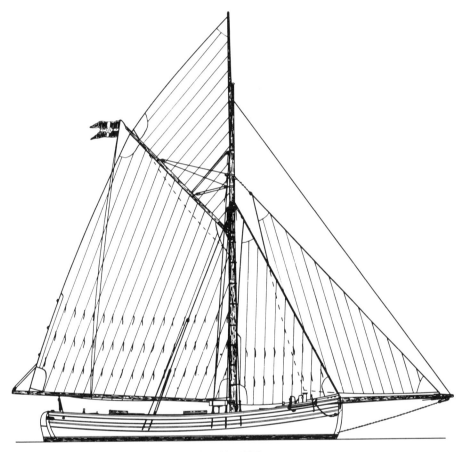

Customs sloop *XXVII* was one of the most recently built customs sloops,
but it was not very different from the earlier ones. It was a splendid
sailer and displayed excellent workmanship throughout.

The sloop was carvel-built of oak and had well-proportioned dimensions. The ribs were alternately single and double, with intervals of
eight and two inches. The rig was gaff with a high topsail and horizontal
jibboom. Aft, there was a locker for various kinds of gear, and forward

there was a cabin for the crew. Amidships there was a cabin with a saloon and an office, and the galley was next to the mast.

Behind the cabin there was a heavy kevel on the stanchions; it was used to make fast the painter to the dinghy, which was always in tow when the sloop was sailing on official business.

The bottom of the sloop had a sheathing of copper, up to nine inches above the waterline. From there to the gunwale it was painted black with a white molding on the lower part of the bulwark. Stanchions, the sides of the cabins, and the winch were painted light yellow, and the skylight, the sliding cover, and the gunwale were unpainted. The cabin roofs and coamings were painted light gray, and the kevels were all unpainted, with the exception of the arms, which were yellow.

Customs sloop *XXV* prior to its being launched at N. F. Hansen's yard at Odense in 1887. Customs sloop *XXVII* resembled very much sloop *XXV*, which is seen with both mast and jibboom in place and with workers and crew on board. The boat's sharp ends and underbody are clearly seen.

Pilot Boat
Helsingør

This pilot boat was built at Helsingør about 1866. Measurement Project
No. 5.

Length: 32 ft 0 in. = 10.04 m
Beam: 11 ft 6 in. = 3.61 m
Height: 4 ft 6 in. = 1.41 m
Draft: ca. 4 ft 0 in. = 1.26 m

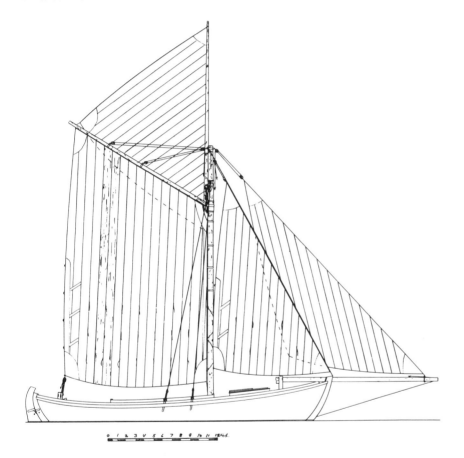

This pilot boat was a strongly built vessel, almost exclusively constructed of oak. It had a gaff rig on a short mast.

The Helsingør pilots often tied up at the Lappegrunden lightship in
order to be closer to the ships coming in from the north as well as to
approach the ships ahead of their Swedish colleagues, who were also
eager to be hired as pilots in that area.

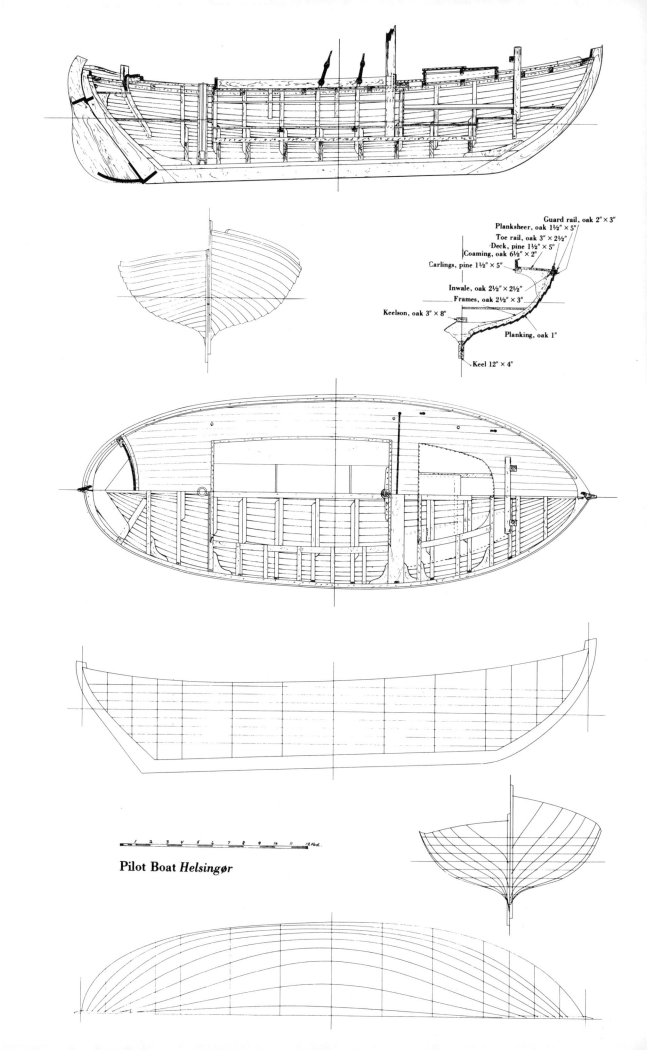

Guard rail, oak 2″ × 3″
Planksheer, oak 1½″ × 5″
Toe rail, oak 3″ × 2½″
Deck, pine 1½″ × 5″
Coaming, oak 6½″ × 2″
Carlings, pine 1½″ × 5″
Inwale, oak 2½″ × 2½″
Frames, oak 2½″ × 3″
Keelson, oak 3″ × 8″
Planking, oak 1″
Keel 12″ × 4″

Pilot Boat *Helsingør*

Boats sailing past Kronborg Castle. One of Helsingør's two pilot boats is seen in the foreground. The boat has no bulwark and has a short mast, and is probably the pilot boat *Helsingør*. Behind *Helsingør* is a cutter or sloop with a swallow-tailed flag. Gouache by Mathias Lütken, 1867.

When the pilot took the hawser from the ship interested in his services, it was brought underneath the bitts and a turn was taken around the posts, since there would be many forceful jerks on the line between the ship and the boat. (The bitts were always strongly built.) The after bitts were used when the pilot boat was tied to the lightship.

The pilot boat had a permanent crew of one, who sailed out with one to four pilots at a time. *Helsingør*, which later was equipped with a motor, was in use until 1941, at which time it was sold to a fish merchant at Ålsgårde.

The bottom of the boat was painted red, the sides were green with a black toe rail, and the coamings were unpainted.

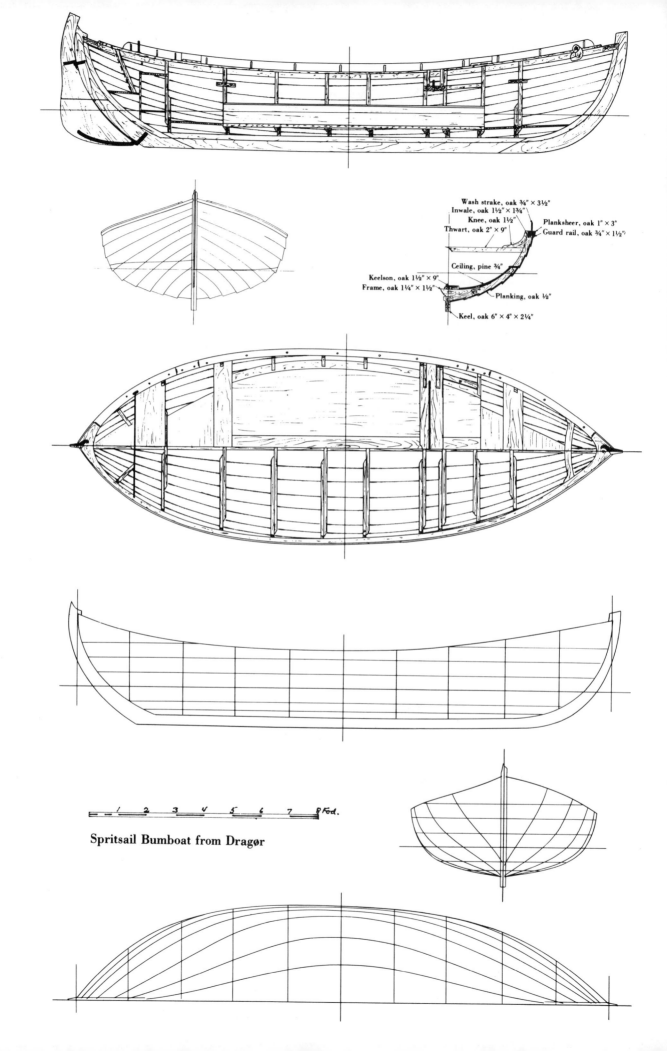

Wash strake, oak ¾" × 3½"
Inwale, oak 1½" × 1¾"
Knee, oak 1½"
Thwart, oak 2" × 9"
Planksheer, oak 1" × 3"
Guard rail, oak ¾" × 1½"
Ceiling, pine ¾"
Keelson, oak 1½" × 9"
Frame, oak 1¼" × 1½"
Planking, oak ½"
Keel, oak 6" × 4" × 2¼"

1 2 3 4 5 6 7 8 Fod.

Spritsail Bumboat from Dragør

Spritsail Bumboat from Dragør

This spritsail craft was built on the Sound in 1888. Measurement Project No. 7.

Length: 18 ft 6 in. = 5.81 m
Beam: 6 ft 4 in. = 1.99 m
Height: 2 ft 3 in. = 0.71 m
Draft: 1 ft 7 in. = 0.50 m

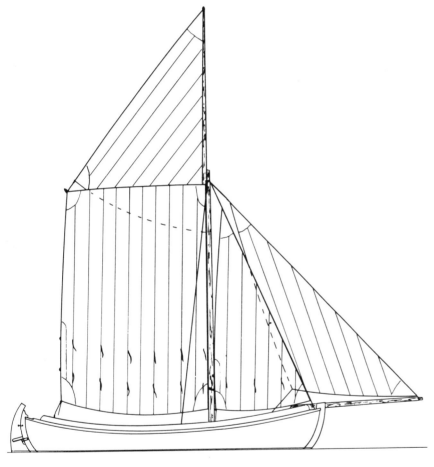

This bumboat was a full but fast craft built of oak. It was equipped with removable washboards at the gunwales, and forward of the mast bench was a thwartships brace, to which was lashed a fender to cushion the impact when the boat came up to the ship in the open sea. Like most of

Ships in the Sound between Rungsted and the island of Hven. An open spritsail boat, which may very well be a bumboat, is approaching a brigantine coming up from the south. Drawing by Christian Blache, 1891.

the other Sound boats, it had a round, curved pinrail to be used in making fast. The boat was also used to fish some herring and flounder, and together with another small boat it was also engaged in searching for old anchors at the bottom of the sea, an effort which provided its owner with some extra income.

The bottom was painted black and the topsides green. The guardrail and the gunwale were gray and the washboards were painted white.

Iceboat from
the Great Belt

This boat was built for the National Railways in 1881. Measurement
Project No. 22.

Length: 21 ft 0 in. = 6.59 m
Beam: 6 ft 8 in. = 2.09 m
Height: 2 ft 8 in. = 0.84 m
Draft: ca. 1 ft 6 in. = 0.47 m

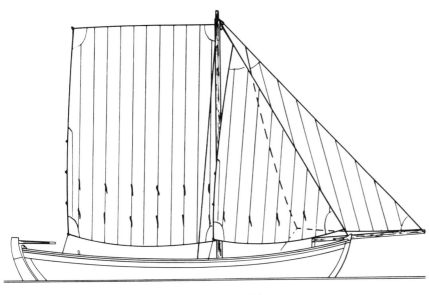

This iceboat is a strong, clinker-built boat constructed entirely of oak.
The boat's ends are round and cut away, making it easy to haul it up on
the sea ice when it is not possible to proceed any further by water.

When the boat was pulled across the ice, it was kept on an even keel
with the aid of the oars, which were placed crosswise under the gunwale
on one side and stuck out on the other, so that the two men who walked
on each side of the boat could use them as levers if the boat tilted over.
The boat was pulled by a long rope fastened through a hole in the stem.
The crew consisted of five or six boatmen, who received a very modest
pay even though the work was considered arduous.

The exterior of the iceboat was painted black with a yellow stripe
below the guardrail, and its interior had a coat of grayish-yellow paint.

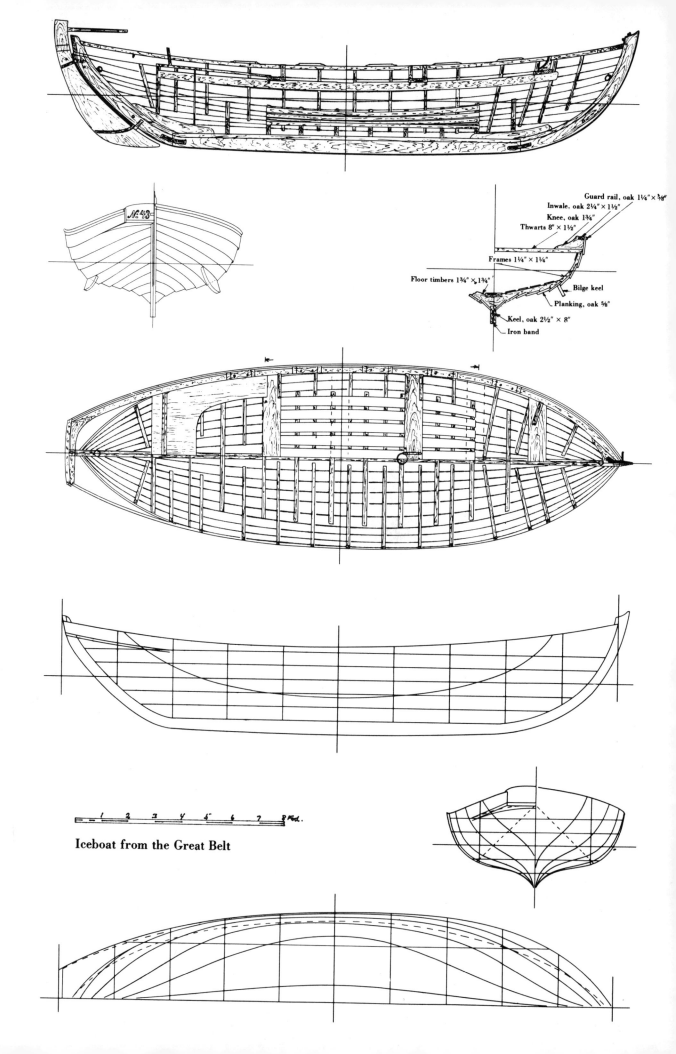

Guard rail, oak 1¼" × ⅞"
Inwale. oak 2¼" × 1½"
Knee, oak 1¾"
Thwarts 8" × 1½"
Frames 1¼" × 1¼"
Floor timbers 1¾" × 1¾"
Bilge keel
Planking, oak ⅝"
Keel, oak 2½" × 8"
Iron band

1 2 3 4 5 6 7 8 Fod.

Iceboat from the Great Belt